Political Columns

BEHIND THE SCENES WITH POWERFUL PEOPLE

By Dr. Allan Bonner, MA, MSc, LLM

Also by the author:

Doing and Saying the Right Thing:
Professional Risk and Crisis Management

Media Relations

Tough Love at the Table
Power, Culture and Diversity in Negotiations,
Mediation & Conflict Resolution

An Ounce of Prevention
Damage Control and Crisis Response

Speaking, Writing and Presenting in SOCKOs®
Strategic Overriding Communications & Knowledge
Objectives

Political Columns: Behind the scenes with powerful people

First printing, February, 2007

Printed and bound by Motion Creative Printing Inc.,
Carleton Place, Ontario, Canada

Published by Sextant Publishing, Edmonton, Alberta, Canada

© Dr. Allan Bonner

Printed in Canada.

ISBN-13: ISBN 978-0-9731134-4-0

For educational or institutional discounts or for information about
Allan Bonner's seminars and speeches, please contact:
Sextant Publishing, Edmonton, Alberta, Canada
or
www.allanbonner.com
1-877-484-1667

TABLE OF CONTENTS

TABLE OF CONTENTS CONTINUED

FOREWORD

Politics is a different kettle of fish, complete with its own brand of spices. It takes a strong character to play in this age-old game effectively, and still have energy at the end of the day to write about it all.

All the players in this game must have a goal and a strategy. Part of the trick is to know what the parameters and limitations you are working within are, then find a way to override and overcome them. This seems to be Allan Bonner's specialty. I've never known him to be held back by any obstacle.

I met Allan at a conference several years ago, and immediately understood him to be a high-energy, results-driven professional, with a keen understanding of the media, political research, public speaking, legislation and how all political tools work. With his unique experience in public affairs, especially in campaigning for office, and staying in office, I was curious to see what kind of writing he could produce for our magazine, *Winning Campaigns*, the largest direct circulation monthly magazine in the political world.

Since our meeting, Allan has been a regular contributor. It is always interesting to see his perspective on different issues, especially contentious matters that other people tend to shy away from because of their complexities. Allan seems to see complex matters as just another challenge that he can sink his teeth into.

I was pleased to learn that Allan is publishing this book with his thoughts and sage advice. The columns in this publication offer words of advice that can be used by anyone who is in the public eye, not just politicians.

It is an excellent overview for those people who want to learn a little bit about what it takes to be in the public life, or for people just looking for a good read. This book tackles countless details about political life, and includes anecdotes from Allan's dealings with leaders throughout the world. Allan shares with us what it takes to be a public figure.

This book is a must have for anyone who is thinking of running for office, who is interested in getting involved in politics, or for anyone who wants a better understanding of what it truly takes to be a successful elected official.

Alan Locke

Winning Campaigns

Falls Church, Virginia

PREFACE

This book has many parents. As a journalist working my way through grad school, I had a steady stream of politicians on my radio and TV programs. There was a great synergy between this *realpolitik* and academic work.

But the real impetus was a series of similar requests over a period of 25 years.

One of the first was from *Law Times*, a periodical for lawyers which asked that I write a regular column on communications issues of interest to lawyers. Politicians, being law makers, became an occasional focus. I attended political meetings and conventions, and wrote about politicians' abilities to speak, motivate and shepherd public policy issues. I contributed for several years.

About this time, I had the good fortune to meet Colin Robertson, son of the CBC television producer, Don Robertson. I'd worked with Don during my time in journalism and found his son to be an equally eclectic gentleman. He is a diplomat and, when we met, was editor of the magazine *Bout de Papier*. As we chatted in my office at TVOntario, he was, unknown to me, looking over my bookshelf. A week later he called saying:

"You seem to read the kind of books I read. Why not write a book review for us?"

This began a series of guest columns on books and issues of interest to international diplomats and trade officials.

Rounding out my experience is a regular column for the largest circulation political magazine in America—*Winning Campaigns*.

I had spoken at a conference with publisher Alan Locke, and when he returned to Virginia, he sent an email asking for a contribution or two. This blossomed into dozens of columns over several years—the main inspiration for this book.

More recently, I was asked to be a regular commentator on elections for the Newsworld TV program "Politics" with Don Newman. This started out as some pre-election commentary on leaders' general abilities. Then, when the election was called, I was asked to comment on developments as they arose—debates, negative ads, the leaders' tours and so on. This blossomed into twice weekly appearances at times.

So, when "Politics" asked for a review of party web-sites, I spent seven hours one weekend reading them. When they wanted a commentary on candidates' speaking styles, I used peer-reviewed academic criteria and a quantitative matrix to review both the speeches and the debates.

As a television viewer and reader of political commentary, I was often disappointed with the unsubstantiated personal or partisan opinion I encountered. I knew this was not helpful to the audience, or sustainable. As a role model, I had in my mind David Gergen's non-partisan television commentaries. Mr. Gergen has worked for Presidents from both parties, and was one of my lecturers at a Harvard course in leadership.

As a result of the considerable research I did for the television commentaries, I had material left over. It was this material that fed two other communications vehicles. First, I blogged several commentaries per week. When I alerted my list of clients and contacts to the information on the blog, I was occasionally asked to write up the concepts for a newspaper or magazine. In the perfunctory words of one editor, "that's great, can you turn it into 750 words?" I did, and more columns appeared in *The Globe and Mail, The Ottawa Citizen, The National Post, The Hill Times* and *The Calgary Herald.*

Finally, my blog afforded me an opportunity to conduct a bit of an experiment. My clients in the military were interested in both the war-time and civilian application of blogs. In a theatre of war, a blog can save lives. If a couple of hundred troops blog that they've seen an airplane that is "one of ours", that's pretty good data and thus not a good idea to blow the plane out of the sky.

Some think that the peace-time and civilian application is to circumvent the mainstream media. When I was asked about this, I resisted the temptation to go along with the agenda. I recognize that most people who have to deal with reporters find them a necessary evil, and many would love to figure out a way around them.

But my research showed that this is both premature and a misreading of what's happening in communications technology. First, I view most media developments in terms of the fragmentation of the market, not in terms of new media technology. Viewers, listeners and readers are leaning away from the three old TV networks in America, not necessarily to experience a new piece of technology—after all, video on a hand-held or computer screen is indistinguishable from that on a cathode ray TV or a flat screen TV. Sure, the medium is the message, as theorist Marshall McLuhan famously said. So, hand-helds are portable, and computer blogs are interactive—but information is information.

The mainstream media aren't dead yet, despite millions of fewer consumers. There is something still validating about being interviewed for a major wire service or "NBC Nightly News". That's what my blog did. It drove the mainstream media to the topics I thought were worth covering during elections. It also drove BBC, CBC, Radio New Zealand, National Public Radio, Global Television and others to my site and then to me.

As final background, I've also worked for many politicians. Right out of grad school, I was full-time executive assistant and speechwriter to the longest serving big city mayor in the world. As a consultant, I then served eight heads of government, a dozen party leaders, three dozen cabinet level officers and several hundred other politicians standing for election. These politicians were in Asia, the Caribbean, Europe and North America.

Some of these columns deal with senior civil servants, diplomats and trade officials. They have similar challenges. They, like politicians, have constituencies, imperatives, power plays and media looking over their shoulders. These clients were in NATO, at G8 meetings, in UN delegations and handling some of the great issues of our time: the disintegration of the former Soviet Union, 9/11, Hong Kong's return to China, European Union, Kosovo, both Gulf Wars and other challenges.

Many of these columns were written while flying to assignments on five continents. I have tried to select those that address recurring themes. The italicized introduction to some columns offers context where I think it's needed. The identities of some subjects have been disguised to protect their privacy and to maintain my sworn confidentiality.

I hope these stories add to the political discourse.

Allan Bonner
Castiglione Falletto, Piedmont, Italy

CARING, KNOWLEDGE AND ACTION

America is so polarized that I have to be careful about writing only about Democrats or Republicans in Winning Campaigns. *I'm in constant danger of alienating 50 per cent of the readership. Below, I had the good fortune to be able to use both Presidents Clinton and Reagan to illustrate a similar point.*

There are a few secret weapons in this column that every political candidate can use. Ronald Reagan had one in spades. So did Bill Clinton.

It's empathy. The ability to understand and identify with another person's emotional state is a powerful tool—especially in politics. This tool doesn't cost a dime either.

Remember Ronald Reagan helping to heal the nation after the space shuttle Columbia explosion? Remember Bill Clinton saying "I feel your pain" and being believed by most? Neither had to display any particular knowledge of the challenging issue at hand, nor unveil any new policy—caring and being seen to care was enough at the time.

One of the best ways to illustrate the power of this secret weapon is to study Ronald Reagan. During his terms in office, some academic research indicated that a majority of Americans questioned the President's expertise. We now know he was a prolific reader and writer, but at the time, he was viewed as not much of a deep thinker. This might be unfair, but that's what the research said.

However, where President Reagan excelled was in expressing, even embodying, empathy and caring for issues and the American people. His pleasant face and demeanor, as well as his "aw shucks" delivery didn't hurt any. Reagan's style caused the electorate to continually give him the benefit of the doubt—on military spending, the deficit, troop casualties in Lebanon, Iran Contra and other issues.

To fully understand how powerful a weapon Ronald Reagan wielded, we need to consult research which shows that expressing caring and empathy can account for up to 50 per cent of a speaker's impact. Knowledge and expertise can be as low as 15 per cent. So, mastering your file and studying the issues is great, but you need that human touch too.

But there's good news for everyone in the research. Taking decisive action or being perceived as highly intelligent can also work in your favor.

In order to understand just how these other traits can work for a candidate, it's useful to look at two of Ronald Reagan's contemporaries on the world stage. They are Margaret Thatcher, his conservative soul mate in the UK, and liberal Pierre Trudeau in Canada, perhaps Reagan's polar opposite in style and substance.

Prime Minister Thatcher transformed the United Kingdom with privatization, and a range of governance and restructuring initiatives. A grocer's daughter of modest origins, she was not known as an intellect or for being particularly empathetic. But she was known for having an ambitious agenda which she pursued doggedly. She was a person of action.

President Reagan's and Margaret Thatcher's terms overlapped for a bit, with the President famously referring to her as the "best man" in Britain. They both overlapped with Canada's Pierre Trudeau—definitely a different character.

Trudeau was in power for most of the years between 1968 and 1984. Watergate tapes have Richard Nixon saying, "That asshole Trudeau is something else". (As a matter of trivia, Reagan was at least a half a foot taller than Trudeau. On a Presidential visit to Canada, Trudeau found two of the tallest Royal Canadian Mounted Police officers in the famous red serge uniform to put the President's height in context).

Unlike Reagan or Thatcher, Pierre Trudeau grew up in great privilege. His father was a multi-millionaire and Pierre went to the best schools and dabbled in post-graduate work in the US and Europe. He bummed around the world long before it was fashionable.

Perceived as cold and distant, Trudeau was not known as a man of action, having really gotten down to work late in life and not doing much of anything in his first term in office. But he was known as a towering intellect—a philosopher king. (His young wife – half his age – once complained of being bored. "Read Plato" was his advice).

But, these three leaders were highly successful, winning re-election repeatedly and relatively easily. They each received varying portions of admiration, respect, and affection.

So the real secret weapon in this column is not just the notion of expressing empathy and caring for issues and people. That may be the easy card to play for some. It doesn't take much research, you just have to dig down deep and determine what you care about.

And it's also the notion that you can succeed by having a full and successful agenda—being a person of action. Or you can also succeed by being highly intelligent and showing it.

Imagine, though, if you combined all three traits. Imagine a President Reagan who had been able to transmit how widely he read and how much of his own speeches he'd personally written. Imagine if he'd also had Margaret Thatcher's political will and action on issues like the deficit and poverty? What if Prime Minister Trudeau could have transmitted Ronald Reagan's caring or been as active as Margaret Thatcher?

Ah. These dreams are the ones that keep new candidates coming forward and campaign teams working hard.

HONEST BOB STANFIELD WAS A CLASS ACT ALL THE WAY

Robert Stanfield refused to engage in the kind of media bashing so popular today.

The theme in this column is universal and timeless—a politicians' rapport with the press. Was a politician's career ruined by one bad photo printed on the front pages of most major dailies in mid-campaign?

No campaign ever hinges on one or two events or policies. The unflattering picture of a national candidate fumbling a football has to be seen in the context of his policies, the attractiveness of his opponent, the skill of his campaign team and that wonderful, intangible moment in history that all the players occupy that causes an election to tip one way or another.

Looking back on this reasonably recent column, I realize how much the matter needs to be footnoted for current readers. Robert Stanfield has become known as 'the best Prime Minister Canada never had'. This may be retrospective appreciation for his character and honesty, but may also be a little angst over what Pierre Trudeau, who beat him, failed to accomplish in his first mandates.

Was Robert Stanfield too decent a man for politics?

The conservative former Premier of Nova Scotia on Canada's East Coast was overwhelmed in 1968 by what came to be called Trudeaumania. A forty-nine year old law professor and writer, Pierre Trudeau swept the country. There was a euphoria after the World's Fair, Expo 67, had been held in Montreal. Canada was briefly on the world stage and liked it. Liberal leader Trudeau seemed to be an international intellectual, suited to keep Canadians there. Ironically, he swept away an era dominated by conservative prairie populist, John Diefenbaker, really the only previous messianic Canadian politician to achieve unprecedented electoral success. Trudeau succeeded his own party's Nobel Prize winning diplomat-statesman Lester Pearson. The irony is that all were well-educated and intelligent. Diefenbaker had a stellar court-room career as a lawyer and was awarded a Master's degree when they were pretty rare. Pearson had been a university lecturer, world class athlete, diplomat and senior civil servant. Stanfield had been an editor of the Harvard Law Review. *Yet all looked stodgy and plodding compared with Trudeau.*

In the 1972 election, Trudeau and Stanfield fought a second contest. On election night, it appeared that Stanfield might win. Many voters went to sleep after midnight thinking they'd wake up to a new Prime Minister.

But, in the end, Trudeau prevailed by a couple of seats and led a compromise, minority government for two years.

Robert Stanfield's grimacing face has been staring down at me from my wall for about 25 years. He looks as if he's in pain as he grabs his own hands instead of the football that appears not only to have slipped through his fingers, but may have also hit him in the groin.

Media folklore has it that this picture helped Stanfield to lose his third election and deny Canada 'the best Prime Minister we never had'. Media bashers say a hostile press, captivated by Pierre Trudeau's suave athleticism, deliberately picked an unflattering shot to portray the Conservative leader as awkward. But, pump a few drinks into a reporter of that era and s/he'll blame the staffer who threw the ball at the candidate.

But, if you dig deep enough, the media comes out looking pretty good on the issue. I wanted to get to the bottom of whether the media were malicious or a staffer was incompetent, so I went down to the offices of The Canadian Press wire service years ago and within minutes had, in my hands, all the negatives from the entire roll of film shot that day in North Bay, Ontario, during the 1974 election campaign. Assuming normal camera settings, I was looking at over a dozen moments, lasting about one-sixtieth of a second, frozen in time for decades. The entire event on the runway may have taken 5 or 10 minutes and only a dozen or so pictures were taken. Those two facts alone constitute a kind of media distortion. The fact that only one picture was picked for the front pages of newspapers is yet another distortion.

However, after studying the entire roll and comparing each picture with the fumbling one that made the newspapers, I became convinced that the picture was very representative of what happened on the tarmac that day. In fact, in the same frame as the fumbling picture, I have the best shot of the day. Mr. Stanfield is catching the ball in mid-stride. But his eyes are closed, his face grimacing as if he'd just eaten a pickle, and he's holding the ball as if it were a wet diaper.

So, on balance, of all the pictures available, the photo editors chose a pretty representative shot to print.

Also in the same frame as these two pictures is a hand-written note from Mr. Stanfield. While doing research on the media at York University in the 1980s, I wrote to him with proposals to clean up media coverage of politics. These proposals were of the kind only an angry young student could dream up. Mr. Stanfield was gracious, indulgent and modest in his hand-written reply.

"I am not very competent to comment on your suggestions. I see some of the things wrong at present but I have not the background to suggest what should be done". After this self-effacing start, he began offering an economical and thoughtful reaction to my version of what was wrong with the media. His most important point was that "it is sometimes hard to get a campaign in focus early enough if journalists report answers to their own questions rather than what the politician wants to emphasize. There ought to be some flexibility".

Mr. Stanfield ended by saying, "I think that, while your suggestions are useful, we haven't really got the answers yet". What a gentlemanly way of reacting to my certain solutions to complex problems.

Even after having an uneasy relationship with television and media performing, Mr. Stanfield refused to engage in the kind of media bashing that people who comment on the fumbling football photo do. He was a gentleman, endured the adamant opinions of a young academic well, and remained circumspect on his own dealings with the press. No wonder he was known in Nova Scotia as "Honest Bob".

SCARY HILLARY

A recent poll says Hillary Clinton is the "scariest" Democratic Presidential candidate. I was asked to do a television commentary on this development, so I started thinking about what this news might mean.

First, I always want to know who commissioned the poll. Are they independent, academic and objective? In this case, at least one of the sponsors of the poll is known to be supportive of the current Republican administration, so I began discounting the results.

Next, I really want to know the methodology. The phrasing, ordering and length of time it takes to ask questions all play a role in the outcome. In most cases I and the public don't get to find out about methodology, so I discounted the results a little more. The dirtiest kind of polling is "push" polling where the phrasing of the question demands a certain kind of answer. Example:

"Are you in favor of freedom and liberty?"

"Did you know Candidate X voted for 17 bills to limit freedom and liberty?"

"If an election were held today would you vote for Candidate X?"

These kinds of polls border on seditious. If you don't favor banning them on freedom of speech grounds, then those who commission them should at least be required to publish their exact questions.

In the Hillary poll, I next wondered what respondents might really be saying by agreeing with the word "scary". They probably didn't use the word, but were asked to agree or disagree with the word as used in concert with candidates' names.

Example:

"On a scale of 1 to 5 where 5 is the most and 1 is the least, how scary are the following candidates?"

So, the respondents weren't the first to use the word "scary"—it was essentially put in their minds and mouths.

They meant something by agreeing to allow the word "scary" to stand. But, we shouldn't be too quick to jump to conclusions about exactly what is meant. Research shows that lay people (in this case not-political scientists) may express themselves in different and non-scientific ways. But they may still be as exact and relevant as elites are in their discussions.

"Scary" is surely a negative descriptor, but I would still discount half the responses if the survey polled the general population. The electorate is so evenly divided that fifty per cent of respondents could just be Republicans who wouldn't say anything nice about any Democrat.

However negative "scary" is, people are probably not referring to how Barry Goldwater was "scary" in 1964. Some were concerned he'd use nuclear weapons in Vietnam, in part thanks to the Democrats' famous "daisy" ad which started with a little girl picking petals off a flower and ending in a mushroom cloud.

Fast forward to this election and the nation is already in an unpopular war, so respondents can't be worried about President Hillary starting or even stepping up conflict. Are they worried about her deficit spending? Hardly, considering the recent Democratic and Republican records in that department.

In this case, I bet "scary" is a surrogate or code word for a number of obvious things. First, there are all those who don't feel we're ready for a woman President. How you get ready for a woman President is another question, but that's how some people put it. Most of this is pure and simple sexism.

Then there's Hillary's personality. Lots of New Yorkers like her, but New York is a welcoming city and jurisdiction. It welcomed Bobby Kennedy as a parachute candidate, as it did Hillary. There's no reason to believe that her voter appeal in New York will translate into votes in the rest of the country.

But Hillary is painted as "frosty" on the late night talk shows.

Letterman says global warming is so bad, Hillary's starting to thaw. This is a more dangerous criticism for her campaign than the ill-defined word "scary". When voters say "Yes" in the voting booth, they are inviting that candidate into their living rooms, via television, for the next four years. Voters must feel comfortable with that candidate. That candidate needs to be comfortable in her own skin.

Hillary's not quite there. If she walked into a Kiwanis meeting in downtown middle-America, she would stand out. She would seem successful, confident, but not quite one of the people. This could be interpreted as out of touch and aloof. She must address this to have a successful Presidential campaign.

Finally, think back to President Carter. He lost the 1980 election for lots of reasons—Iran, the economy, Three Mile Island—you can add to the list. But in addition to all the issues you could name, there was one other human factor that pollsters probably didn't ask about and respondents didn't express.

That factor was simply that large segments of the country got sick of Jimmy Carter and his family. They were sick of his accent, Amy, his mother and especially his brother Billy who toured the country selling Billy Beer and attending belly flop festivals in hotel pools.

Hillary should be worried about whether the country got sick of the Clintons in the same way. For more than eight years we had Bill and his proclivities, their unconventional marriage and even the silly issue of her not baking cookies.

Even the old notion, that with Hillary we get Bill for free, might work against her. The good news is we get Bill, and the bad news is ... we get Bill.

The most dangerous aspect of voters being sick of the Clintons may involve their unconventional marriage. It certainly doesn't appear to be a Christian Right kind of marriage, or even a compassionate conservative kind of marriage, despite the fact that infidelity surely plagues those groups as much as it does the general population.

"Scary" could just stand for a partisan assessment of how well the Clinton's lifestyles fit into conservative thinking. And that takes us back to how polarized the electorate is these days. In this environment, Hillary has to work hard on her image, and voters have to work to see through surrogate issues reported in polls.

Research Design Issues

I have many concerns about the quality of research conducted in political campaigns, by those governing and by industrialists. I even see those in the not-for-profit sector spending precious money on unproductive research.

"Original" research in universities is often only conducted at the doctoral level. Research that is done often involves relatively unproductive statistical tables or questionnaires that purport to be "scientific". Many students find searching through microfilm, microfiche and original texts in libraries to be passé, if they are aware of the technique at all. This constricted research in universities translates into marginally beneficial or even irrelevant techniques and results in industry and government.

How is it that the best educated generation the world has ever seen is relying on research techniques that would not achieve a pass in a second year social science course in a reputable university? In government, and in the political campaigns designed to lead to governing, senior managers are making decisions based on flawed methodology.

But we are in unstable times when we need excellent public policy and politics. America is polarized domestically and the European Union is beginning to show signs of eventually having economic and political clout similar to the U.S.

For those who look to the private sector for leadership and use the refrain of "running the government like a business"—please don't. Fully 82 per cent of all mergers and acquisitions in private industry fail to produce new value. There is a crisis of competence in all sectors, in part because of poor research.

Here are the top ten issues and comments on research techniques and challenges faced both in campaigns and then in governing:

1) Polls

The population is much more sophisticated than they were when the random sample telephone survey was invented. A telephone call is now an intrusion, especially during dinner time. Pollsters are experiencing up to 70 per cent refusal rates. I tell my clients that often the biggest message they are getting is that their constituents refuse to speak to them at all.

Compounding the problem is caller ID which tips people off that it's a pollster calling. The moment of silence before the questioner begins speaking is a further tip off, as is the robotic reading of questions from a computer screen.

Perhaps the biggest challenge is that up to 10 per cent of the population has just one hand-held device or phone—higher in the crucial 18-24 age group. Many will not participate in phone surveys because they have to pay the air time.

People have inaccurate memories of dates, events and attitudes— what researchers call "backward and forward telescoping". They also tell researchers what they wish had happened, or use answers to researchers' questions as surrogates for other messages. The classic example is that far more Americans reported that they voted for President Kennedy after his assassination than could have done so in the closest election the US had had to that date.

Social science is too imprecise to determine that 22.3 per cent of people think or do anything—often referred to as "spurious accuracy".

Citizens reserve the right to lie to pollsters and reserve the right to park their votes in the undecided category or tell pollsters they will vote for a party or candidate when they have no intention of doing so, in order to temporarily reward or punish candidates.

One joke about polls goes like this: "If an election were held today, everybody would be really surprised because it's scheduled for November 4". That kind of captures some of the unreality of polls these days.

2) Focus Groups

Robert K. Merton is the inventor of focus groups. He also coined the terms "role model" and "self-fulfilling prophecy". He disassociated himself from the way practitioners implemented his ideas about focus groups.

The dirty little secret about focus groups is the number of times companies rely on semi-professional attendees whom they know will show up on short notice to fulfill a client's needs. Students, the disadvantaged and others who need an honorarium or have time on their hands are often overrepresented.

There are ways to make focus groups more reliable. What the *Harvard Business Review* calls "empathic testing", involves using a product or discussing an issue in real life conditions. Putting respondents around a board room table and having a formal focus group leader ask questions is not a normal life experience or venue and the results will thus be forced and false.

Anamatics is a similar method and involves making the experience realistic and having participants focus on the element to be tested. Realism in the venue can be addressed by driving respondents around in a van while they listen to radio ads a politician wants tested. This is closer to how voters would listen to an ad.

For TV ads, we have stripped rough cut ads into tapes of the actual TV show in which they will appear. Testing can occur in shopping malls where hundreds or even thousands of people can view the potential ads and react to them.

For print ads and even editorial content, we have mocked up the copy and inserted it into real newspapers to see how respondents react. We don't tell them what we want them to react to, we first want to know if they care to look at the ad or story at all. That's the so-called "unaided" response. If they don't look or read, we have some valuable information. Then we ask them to review the ad and get more valuable information in their "aided" response.

Campaigns and sitting politicians use lots of mail. Direct mail raises money and mobilizes troops. Newsletters and political "householders" let constituents know what their representative is doing. But nobody opens the mail or reads a householder while sitting around a board room table. These items should be thrown on the floor in a pile of other mail and magazines to see if anybody bothers to stoop down and pick them up. If someone does, the next question is whether the political piece is interesting enough to cull out of the pile and read. If not, that's a valuable answer in itself.

While on the campaign literature theme, there's always somebody in political meetings showing a mock up of a brochure or householder who points out that the candidate's picture or name or other important information is off on the right-hand side "where the eye naturally goes". By this time in the meeting, I'm too exhausted from trivia and nonsensical issues to point out that we read from left to right in English, Spanish, French and most other languages prevalent in North America, and only read right to left in Arabic, Persian, and some other languages. (I wonder where these perceived and received pieces of communication wisdom come from?)

With regard to video and TV production, audiences are very sophisticated. Most people own video cameras and watch TV dozens of hours per week. Research has shown that focus group attendees will review the production qualities of ads, rather than the content. To counter this, advertisements can be mocked-up by a graphic artist and one can then test the voice-over or content separately.

Candidates can test debate one-liners, still pictures for brochures, slogans and any other communication element, without layers of clutter or testing of extraneous elements.

3) Graduated Questionnaires

Self-administered questionnaires are not used much anymore, but are a valid technique. One of the best examples of these is the old Bureau of Broadcast Measurement diaries that were mailed to households to survey radio listening and TV viewing. People often put down their favorite station, not the one they actually watched most.

With telephone or in-person surveys, respondents become easily and quickly fatigued with having to choose among: strongly agree, mildly agree, somewhat agree, agree, mildly disagree, strongly disagree. What does mildly agree mean, other than the fact that it's stronger than just agreeing and weaker than strongly agreeing? How does one compare one person's strong agreement with another person's?

The best model to determine the weight to put on a respondent's report is to see if that person actually changes behavior as a result. People often report that they will change voting habits, but actually do not. This makes their threat to do so a surrogate for other matters that should be probed.

In industry, it's the same. I have a telecommunications client which conducts quarterly research to determine how much its customers like them. The results show that up to 30 per cent of respondents say they "agree", "strongly agree" or "somewhat agree" with the notion of switching service to a new company. Yet for years the so-called "churn rate"—the rate at which customers actually change telecommunications providers (phones, hand-helds, internet, etc.) is under 3 per cent.

It is vital to distinguish between what people actually do and what they say they might do.

4) Elite Interviews

It may not sound egalitarian these days, but elites are good respondents because of how they became elites—they know their demographic well. These one-on-one, in-depth interviews can augment focus groups, polling and other techniques.

Who's an elite? That's easy. Ratepayer groups, condominium boards, religious groups, union leaders and even book club busy bodies all rose to the top of their little heap, in part through knowing what their demographic is like. They can be a great source of information.

5) Triangulation

The term, taken from navigation, stands for gathering data from several different sources, or with numerous methodologies. Where data intersect, results are more reliable.

Researchers have identified several types of triangulation including: within-method, between-method, data, investigator, theory and methodological triangulation. Within-method means two separate polls, perhaps by different companies that say the same thing.

Between-method might be a poll and a focus group that produce similar results. Data triangulation might involve qualitative or quantitative results that are much the same. If several investigators find out the same thing, that's triangulation. Theory triangulation might involve a psychological and sociological explanation of behavior. Finally, these days, using mixed methods—both qualitative and quantitative—is increasingly the norm to avoid the errors that each alone can produce.

6) Mixed Methods

The distinction between qualitative and quantitative data has been blurred for at least 50 years. Few branches of any science have the predictability of Newtonian physics. Current thinking is to engage in a mixture of the methodologies mentioned above. So, a reproducible poll with a large sample that claims to be "scientifically" accurate might be cross-referenced with qualitative focus groups, elite interviews and such that plumb small samples more deeply.

7) Question Formulation

Average people don't speak the way telephone researchers do, or the way those who write questions think they should. It's hard to imagine anyone constructing a questionnaire where a response could be "some good" which is a common expression in the Canadian Maritimes, or "awesome" as is currently popular. The California "Valley Girl" response of "gag me with a spoon" was probably not used, even in its heyday.

8) Telephone Interviewers

In addition to the long pause, script reading and intrusion, some companies balk at long distance charges, skewing data to urban respondents. For decades, first year social scientists have been warned that telephone surveys obviously only gather information from those with telephones. Triangulation is the antidote.

9) Reflexivity

Social scientists are supposed to keep notes, tapes and a reflexive diary to examine themselves as a scientific instrument while they are examining other people or issues. Commercial researchers would rarely do this.

10) The Heisenberg Uncertainty Principle

The use of a particular research instrument has an effect on the outcome of the research. Heisenberg stated, "[o]n the level of molecular research, the presence of the experimenter is certain to affect the results in a way which cannot be measured".

The mere fact that a pollster calls up respondents has such effect. Asking about certain topics that the respondent might not be concerned with puts that matter on the public agenda. Moreover, researchers cannot control for the myriad other variables in that respondent's life.

In the end, perhaps my premise is flawed. Perhaps we are not the best educated generation the world has ever seen. We have more degrees and a multiplicity of choices in methods, but may lack the clarity and professionalism of previous generations. Pity, we need that clarity.

DEMOCRACY WORKED FOR BOTH SIDES

I still run into voters who say they voted for President Bush in 2004 because he was the lesser of two evils. They did not find that John Kerry had a compelling or coherent platform, but were still not drawn to the incumbent President.

On the mandate issue, one of many referenced in this article, it's interesting that George Bush waited until well into his second term to use his first veto. He found other ways to have his way—through lobbying a friendly Congress or just interpreting laws in the way he saw fit.

During this Presidential election I felt like the sportswriter for one of the great, old New York newspapers. It was during World War II when most able-bodied men were in uniform and major league baseball had a lot of young boys and old men playing. There was even a one-armed ball player. In the field he would catch the ball, throw it up while jettisoning the glove from his hand, catch the ball and throw to the infield. He batted one-armed too.

Anyway, a sportswriter wrote a column that went like this: I've examined these two teams entering the World Series. I've looked at their strengths and weaknesses. I've poured over the statistics. After all this, I've come to the inescapable conclusion that neither one of these teams can win the World Series.

That's how I felt about Bush and Kerry. In fact, in some ways neither did win, but one certainly lost. What follows is a series of observations that are worth mulling over with a coffee, or something stronger.

John Kerry lost because he could not transmit that he is a regular guy. Ever since George Washington was reluctantly persuaded to assume the Presidency, one of the strongest myths in US politics is that it is a little unseemly to campaign actively for the office. It's only in this century where front porch letters of concern by candidates turned into whirlwind jet-speed tours of the States. There's a fine line between being drawn by others to the office and being a tireless campaigner for a cause. Kerry looked too calculated. Also, ever since Abraham Lincoln's log cabin, humble beginnings have also been part of the presidential mythology. America was founded on suspicion of rank, privilege and power and Kerry had lots of each.

I've had a beer and done business in places like Wichita, Deadwood, Bellingham and Sacramento. If George Bush had walked into the saloon, he could have easily passed for the local Chamber of Commerce or Kiwanis type. If John Kerry had walked in, everybody would have wondered who the dude was.

Mandate

Pundits talk about the President getting a mandate as if America had a parliamentary system. In the great parliamentary democracies, the Prime Minister may have fewer members and thus votes than the combined opposition parties. S/he has to make sure the votes are there for a confidence motion, such as a budget. If not, the government falls and there's an election. But, when the President becomes President, he's the President. Period. All Presidents can veto, submit legislation and use their "bully pulpit" as Teddy Roosevelt called it. They also wage war. Truman used the atomic bomb without being elected at all. John Kennedy's Bay of Pigs came after the closest American election in history. Richard Nixon's escalation of the Vietnam war came after his electoral college votes were fewer than Humphrey's and Wallace's put together. George W. Bush went to Iraq after the 2000 election in which he had fewer popular votes than his opponent, Al Gore. The President has a mandate by virtue of being President.

The Government

I've had many martinis at the bar called "701" in Washington on Pennsylvania Avenue in between The White House and The Capitol. A regular question there is "what will the government do?" The best answer is another question—"which government?" There's the government up at 1600 Pennsylvania where the President lives. Then there's the government in the House and the government in the Senate. Sometimes there's the government in the Supreme Court. The country was founded by people who were so distrustful of big government, they designed a system with checks and balances. There are so many checks and balances that paralysis is often a result. But that's OK. The system was designed to not work easily.

Debates

Forty-four years after the first televised debate, pundits still cover them as if they were decisive factors in elections. They never have been. Not even the Nixon-Kennedy debates! Ballot stuffing in Chicago wouldn't have been necessary had Kennedy's winning debate had the effect some say it did.

Senate Speeches

It's pretty obvious that John Kerry has been making boring speeches in the Senate for a lot of years. Unlike the parliamentary system, no President or Senator actually debates anyone. In the Senate, members intone their messages to a neutral Chair and sit down. Then another Senator drones on. It's not good practice for the hustings.

All Four America!

There's the East Coast, the West Coast, and then there's America. I first heard that old line forty years ago. But if you go back hundreds of years, America really had at least four founding factions. There were those who came for religion—to pray the way they wanted to and forbid others from praying in other ways. Others came to colonize. A third group came to trade and make money. A fourth group came to create an agricultural economy. There may be others—adventurers, escapees and such—but four diverse groups are plenty. Is America divided? You bet. But it always has been.

Tribal Divisions

You can overlay these four Americas with the North and the South. But, better still overlay the Christian Right. Forty-six per cent of Americans say they are fundamentalist, evangelical and/or born again. (Yet, one survey found far more Americans claim to go to church than those who actually drive cars on Sundays). Then there are divisions by issue: guns, abortion, gay marriage. Only low single digits of Americans are undecided or switch parties.

National Unity

There are calls for Bush to put a few Democrats in his cabinet to reach out to the other side. This will have a small effect. There are calls for John Kerry to do something to foster unity, and he appears willing. The problem is that he has no role to play. He could be appointed Ambassador to the UN or France, but then he disappears into those black holes, with little effect on middle-America. In the parliamentary system, John Kerry would lead an official, loyal opposition where he would put forth the views of the nearly 50 per cent of voters who supported him. If his party chose another leader, Kerry would still be an opposition critic asking questions every day.

It's a shame there isn't a more constructive role for the losing candidate to play. But there is precedent to appoint John Kerry "ambassador at large" to tour the world, or even put him in cabinet. That would be pretty bold, but this is wartime and coalition or national governments are very common during such times in the parliamentary system and not without precedent in the US.

The System is Flawed

In the old days—the 1960s—an election would be dragging on past the time when all decent folks should have been watching Johnny Carson. Some curmudgeon like David Brinkley would growl that a couple of county clerks from Nebraska could count these ballots faster. Forty years later we have the tyranny of technology in 50 state elections, rather than one, national, Presidential election. It has to be fixed or court decisions on ballots and eligibility will decide elections. Voters will abstain or get really angry if they are put through agony to cast a ballot. This time, some voters waited up to nine hours to vote and that cannot stand.

Churchill

If a magazine called *Winning Campaigns* doesn't feature a quote from Winston S. Churchill every now and then, there's something wrong. He said something like democracy was the worst system of government imaginable, except for every other one you could possibly come up with. He also said that if you're going through hell—keep going. This is good advice for losing candidates.

Network Pandering

When Richard Nixon left The White House in disgrace, most pundits said he did so with dignity and grace. Nonsense! Only Roger Mudd, the best anchor the US networks never had, summoned the courage to remind viewers that the President was leaving in disgrace. Too many pundits and commentators pander to the viewer by going on and on about the world's greatest democracy and the dignity of the candidates. Democracy is messy and nobody has perfected it. The candidates are also angry and bitter following an election loss—don't kid yourself.

Concession Speeches

One of the best I've ever heard of went like this: "The people have spoken... the bastards".

IMAGE CAN MAKE THE DIFFERENCE

BETWEEN WINNING AND LOSING

The mundane issue of not getting a cold during a campaign illustrates the countless little things that can make a difference. I've always marveled at how democracy seems most alive around kitchen tables, especially when there's a phone bank on the go or election day when ordinary people are getting out the vote.

This column capitalizes on my consulting work in that environment. In this case, the leader and his party didn't do well, but he's vowed to battle in the next election, and has asked me to help.

About a year ago I was in the middle of the continent with about a dozen prospective candidates. I said I was going to show them my secret political weapon that had been successful with hundreds of candidates, cabinet officers and heads of government. I pulled out some hand sanitizer from my brief case, which I use when I'm on the road up to 150 days per year.

The fact is, if you shake 1,000 hands, you'll get a cold. Then you'll be either out of the game or performing below optimum for a week. In a short campaign, you can't afford the time off. I advised the candidates to use the sanitizer often, and out of the sight of TV cameras.

Very often, winning campaigns boil down to such mundane issues as hand sanitizer. After all, name recognition, personal contact with voters and image play huge roles in electoral wins.

That last word, "image", is a controversial one for me as I counsel leaders in industry, government and politics. Many have the impression that image is frivolous, like getting your colors done. But academic study shows there is most often a lot of substance behind that apparently superficial image.

Voters in a democracy have no obligation to keep themselves informed. They have a right to, but no obligation. Those who want to be informed are allowed to choose the depth of information they want, the frequency of their searches for information and the media to consume. One citizen may scour conspiracy sites on the Internet, and another subscribe to Foreign Affairs Magazine.

Most readers of this publication know that huge numbers of young voters get their political information from late night TV comedy shows. Superficial, you might think. But I've been a journalist, taught journalism and studied the news media, and I can assure you that David Letterman produces a better interview with political figures on many occasions than do the big time interviewers on "60 Minutes". Jon Stewart on Comedy Central does the same with a little more schtick.

By the way, there's also nothing new about political figures on late night TV. It didn't start with Bill Clinton playing the sax or even Ronald Reagan on Johnny Carson. Richard Nixon was a guest on "Laugh In" and Bobby Kennedy campaigned for JFK on Jack Paar's 'Tonight Show".

Neither is preparing and rehearsing for political appearances new. One of the rabble-rousers in the French revolution hired an actress to make him a better speaker. Demosthenes was his own media trainer in ancient Greece. He put pebbles in his mouth and tried to be heard over roar of waves at the beach, in an effort to become a more compelling speaker.

Those who think democracy is going to hell in a handbasket because of the TV age's preoccupation with image, should be sent to the woodshed to read 19th Century political pamphlets or early 20th Century yellow journalism or even look at the ethical problems early radio and TV stations had. There are many old examples of what could be categorized as libel or even hate crimes.

And those who don't feel it's fair for late night comedians to make fun of political figures should look at the blistering cartoons done by Thomas Nast, which helped topple Tammany Hall figures in

New York in the late 19th Century. They should also consider whether the media circus that flourishes around today's campaigns does democracy any more harm than the smoke filled back rooms that picked candidates before about 1950.

So, preoccupation with image isn't new, and image building isn't necessarily bad. In business, we don't fault an executive who purposefully sets out to add line items to her resumé for future job prospects. Why should we fault the politician who tries to do the same thing?

In fact, academics say that issues are hard for many voters to understand. Moreover, the issues during a campaign may well not be the ones a candidate has to deal with when elected. The academics conclude that image is more easily understood and transmitted than are issues, and image is not too bad a criteria with which to judge candidates.

TV journalists have a simpler way of describing all this: "the camera doesn't lie". Sure, the camera gets fooled some of the time, but Kennedy actually was cool, Ronald Reagan did have a happy disposition, Richard Nixon was tricky and Jimmy Carter was a nice, decent guy in over his head.

So what are the rules of cultivating and transmitting a positive image? First of all, "be yourself" is far too simple and very hard to achieve. If it were simple, why do I make a living helping people with their images? Too many public figures seem to be playing the role they think they should, rather than the one they are committed to. I want to get politicians to think beyond the platitudes in their stock speeches to what they really think, feel and believe. Then, I want them to look as if they think, feel and believe. In cases where they're not sure, I have them draw their messages in stick figures. Pictures are concrete, but words can be vague. Drawing clears the air.

Non-verbal communication though, accounts for between 50 and 75 per cent of a politician's impact. Open, double hand gestures with palms at a 45 degree angle and elbows at 90 degrees is a great start. Leaning into the dialogue by about 2 degrees from the waist shows you're engaged. Slower movements are best for TV. Body language should get bigger for bigger audiences.

Eye contact is vital. If you've ever been to a party where the person you're speaking with is looking over your shoulder for a more important person to chat up, you'll understand how a speaker needs to maintain eye contact. With one person, look as if you are totally engaged and don't take your eyes off her. In a big crowd, move eye contact slowly among people in each quadrant of the room. Stick with one person for a few sentences or points and then move on.

Clothing presents challenges for both male and female politicians. In the heat, you want to stay cool, but linen wrinkles. So-called micro fibers, that even the big Italian designers favor, are basically as cool as wearing plastic. If you can get a mohair and wool blend, it's like having a little steel wool woven in. The mohair keeps a crease but the air blows right through.

The general rule is to dress "one up" from the audience. If it's the Board of Trade lunch, your best suit is in order. If you're campaigning at a factory gate, a blazer and open shirt is still one up. In a farmer's field or soup kitchen, cotton chinos and a plaid shirt might be the choice.

You don't want what you are wearing to distract voters from you and your message. Bracelets, dangling earrings and gold neck chains are usually a distraction. On TV they can create a video "flare" like you see on country and western singer's suits and guitars. Tight patterns such as Harris Tweed, glen check or hound's-tooth can do the same. Men need executive socks and women need longer hem lines for modesty when sitting and getting in and out of cars. Women can approximate the authoritative version of the suit and tie with a jacket, scarf, broach or pearls.

Once a candidate has decided on the right wardrobe, one good trick is to buy three versions of everything. If you're getting in and out of cars, sleeping on planes and tramping through crowds or farmers' fields, you'll be wrinkly and coffee-stained. With three identical outfits, you have one to wear, one being pressed, and one hanging up ready for the next pit stop. Advance people should have scouted out places to change. It puts a damper on the event, if the candidate has just had to change pantyhose in a dingy garage washroom. The locations of dry cleaners for minor repairs and pressing should be on the itinerary, whether they are used or not.

Candidates need to be comfortable. You need to have frank discussions about support hose for men and women, low heels, spongy soles, gel inserts and anything else that can make being on your feet 14 hours a day bearable. Socks should be changed mid-day and shoes daily to prevent blisters and fatigue. Whatever will allow the candidate to sleep must be procured, such as eye shades, ear plugs, white noise machines or neck pillows.

In the end, a fresh, pressed, bright candidate who can work an extra hour a day without falling asleep or telling a reporter to "shove it" can make the difference on election day. Victory is in the details.

$$$ MAKES THE POLITICAL WORLD GO AROUND

BUT PROPER TECHNIQUE BRINGS THE DOLLARS IN

There's too much money in American politics.
Everybody knows that. But I don't have a solution.
So I present this technical article on raising money
without the companion piece that's needed—how to
run a democracy on an affordable budget.

Money is the mother's milk of politics, they say. Well, I know a little something about milking—real cows that is.

You have to nuzzle your head in the soft crux between the cow's back leg and stomach. You tie off the top of the teat with a firm squeeze between the thumb and index finger, as if you're making the "OK" sign. Then you roll down the teat with the middle, ring and baby finger, successively, in a smooth motion. Repeat with the other hand on another teat.

Real pros can get a rhythm going and chew tobacco between squeezes. They can also get a little tune going with the sound the high speed milk makes as it hits the side of the bucket. The notes change as the bucket fills up.

I live in the big city now. But the mother's milk of politics is just as hard to extract as real milk. To make matters worse, techniques change over the years, as if cows and hands and teats changed shape.

Traditional fundraising dinners are great. I once worked for a politician who held a $15,000 a plate dinner with white gloves on the waiters and no media. The next year it was $1.49, but you were expected to make a big donation. Depending on the tax structure, the Christmas basket or Thanksgiving turkey that you buy for $100.00 and get a tax receipt for $75.00 can work really well. A strategic alliance with the grocery store helps.

In succession, snail mail, the phone, the fax and email have all lost some of their bite. At least they need fine tuning. There was a time that massive mail outs in the millions could fund a great campaign on a two per cent return. But those were the days of "the more you tell, the more you sell". Two page letters that started with bland philosophical notes don't work any more. Too many letters begin like this: "Now that the new year is upon us, we must all set new goals and scan new horizons. Like you, I am concerned about the future of our communities".

Whoever sends me this gets a one way ticket to the garbage.

Speed dialers that cause a short pause after I answer the phone make me hang up. So does an 800 number on call display. I no longer get hundreds of junk faxes, but I still get hundreds of emails. I employ someone to delete them, so a fundraising message better be appealing to that person, not me.

But it's not all bad news. People want to be involved in politics. Many who don't have time will give money or goods in kind. Reaching them is the issue. Years ago I got involved in politics because a friend of mine ran for office. I had a Rolodex of contacts from outside politics. I had fantastic success selling tickets to fundraisers to people who had never been approached before.

One day a woman wandered into the campaign office and we pounced on her, offering coffee and telling her how great the candidate was. She said she just thought the place was for rent and wanted to run a kid's gym class in it. Although she had no interest in politics to that date, we recruited her. She raised a bundle of money by bringing in her new Rolodex as well.

My most successful event came after a brainstorming session with the finance committee. We decided that we'd hold the event in someone's home to save money. But whose? Somebody knew that multi-millionaire cable magnate and current owner of Skydome and the Toronto Blue Jays, Ted Rogers, had a nice home.

"Yeah, but whose going to call him?" Somebody asked. As the Young Turk, I offered. I really lucked out because I was an executive at a TV network and Mr. Rogers is known as a hands on guy who actually returns his own phone calls. Perhaps he also thought I had some legitimate business with his cable company.

He called back the same morning and took 25 seconds to agree to lend us his home. I sold 135 tickets. The cost of the event was a few bucks a person for snacks and drinks and the profit was huge. The draw was Mr. Rogers' home and perhaps the candidate—the double whammy!

Whether it's asking for money or selling tickets, telephone volunteers need a connection to the issue, the candidate or preferably the person they're calling. I can just hear the pages of the telemarketing script go by: "Hello, Mr. Bonner. How are you this evening?" "Fine". "That's great. I'm just calling to thank you and your family for your generous support in past years for (insert political cause, institution or candidate). We're running a charity hockey game this year. Are you a hockey fan?"

On and on this goes, like the old two page telemarketing letters. Even people who went to my universities are wasting their time chatting me up like this.

I made $5,000 per night calling parents of my kid's school with a 15 second pitch like this: "Hello, it's Allan Bonner. I'm a school parent and your son Jeff is in the same class with my boy Michael. Each year I volunteer to raise money for the school. Tuition only covers about 80 per cent of school activities and a lot of us want the rest to be deductible, directable and discretionary. How much can I put you down for?"

If there was a protest about having no money, I'd say any amount would be great, just so I could report 100 per cent giving from the class parents. Some groaned and gave me $25 and some $3,000.

My surprising rule then is—ask!

Don't get me wrong. There are pros out there that can help you with push-polling, slicing demographics, fake lobby campaigns (astro-turf vs. grass roots) and such. But in most campaigns, it's volunteer armies that win the battles. That army needs low overhead, new blood and simple techniques.

"Pressing the Flesh"

Vital Part of Campaigning

I've had the privilege of knocking on many thousands of doors with winning and losing candidates. Best practices include: getting people to actually open the door; getting candidates to disengage in a long conversation; and covering lots of real estate quickly.

In a tall building, I watch the candidate at the last door on a floor. As the conversation is winding down, I run down the stairs to the next floor and take the chance of knocking on the first two doors across the hall from each other. I assume one person is out and I'll get one live body for my trouble. I proceed in the same way down the hall as the candidate arrives on this new floor.

Street campaigning presents different challenges. The principle is still to charge through lots of real estate and get live bodies at the door. I try to hop ahead of the candidate and like at least two teams of two going down each side of the street. But canvassers have to avoid interrupting lawn or car care.

One joke among political canvassers is that the average person in an apartment takes his or her

clothes off immediately upon arriving home,
whereas homeowners wait until after dinner. Most
of us have stories about being greeted by men and
women in towels, housecoats, or less.

Some of my canvassers and I have helped students
move in a couch. We've done minor repairs and
refused drinks. All of us have had to use creativity
to pull the candidate away from a talkative, parti-
san or lonely voter. The easiest is to indicate a
neighbor is waiting for the candidate next door.

But, the next column features a lesson I learned
about the geography of the political district. I guess
you could spend a lifetime in politics and still learn
a new trick or two in your last campaign.

Local conditions always apply in politics. You'd think door-to-door campaigning would be much the same everywhere, but I've seen quite a few variations, depending on the geography.

In the prairies, you drive farm to farm, and one of the big tricks is getting out of the kitchen after only two or three cups of coffee. And, if you're chatting up a farmer working on his combine in the field, you better be able to help out while you talk.

In Connecticut, the homes are so far apart candidates worry about losing time driving between them. Unlike prairie farming communities though, Connecticut residents have to take their garbage to a dump. Saturday is the preferred day, so candidates gladhand and give out literature at the dump entrance. And some say politics has lost its glamour…

Urban campaigning is either in high rise buildings or residential streets. In apartments or condos, the first trick is getting in. Buzzing one resident and citing some obscure law that allows candidates to canvass the building will often do the trick. In fact, many tenant-landlord acts do have such a provision. Most often, a resident is pretty flattered when you say a version of the following:

"Hello, my name is Allan Bonner and I'm here with (name party) candidate John Smith meeting with some neighbors and I just wonder if you have a few minutes to say 'hi' to him?"

Sometimes the superintendent or doorman will let you in too. In some buildings you should book the party room in advance and plan a little event, complete with coffee and cookies.

The introduction you use partly depends on how the election is going. With a candidate who has strong name recognition, polling ahead of the party, you may just want to keep saying you're with John Smith. If it's the reverse, mention the party. Sometimes it's the fact your local candidate is a big supporter of, or supported by, the Governor or President that is worth a try. Literature will reflect these realities too.

Once in the building, the next trick is to get people to open the door. Wearing a campaign button and holding a piece of literature clearly identifies you as a political canvasser. The best technique is to knock loudly on the door, step back a full pace, and when the door opens a crack, say the following in a clear, loud voice:

"Hello, I'm your neighbor Allan Bonner, and I'm here with John Smith who's running for re-election. He's meeting with some of your neighbors today and I hope you have a minute to say 'hello' to him".

At this point, you look down the hall of the building hoping the candidate is disengaging from another door. You are speaking in a loud voice to signal to the rest of the canvass team that you have a live voter on the hook. If you're working with a two to four person team and the candidate, you should be able to leapfrog over doors with no one home and keep finding people for the candidate to speak with. When no one's home, you leave a personally written note: "Sorry I missed you when I called".

Be careful. I've seen campaigns where a candidate stood up at the debate and showed off half a dozen pieces of his opponent's literature with different signatures and writing styles. He asked if the electorate should trust a guy who won't sign his own name?

In condos and apartments you still have the problem of people who won't open the door. I developed a technique that usually breaks the ice. After knocking, I step back and watch the peep hole. When the person inside looks through to see who's there, it goes dark as the eye presses up against it. At this exact moment I begin speaking: "Oh hi! My name is Allan Bonner, and I'm here with (etc.)".

For a brief moment, many people mistakenly think I can see them because they can see me and I'm speaking to them. They answer when I ask how they are and whether they've met the candidate. They are now pretty well committed to opening the door.

All of candidate canvass is designed to increase contact, the perception of being in the neighborhood, and name recognition. In the voting booth, all this can be worth up to ten per cent of the vote.

A good canvass team can move a candidate through a high rise very quickly. You sometimes have to rescue the politician from a talkative voter. A worker can jump in with a comment, offer to take down the constituent's concerns and speak on the phone later, or simply tell the candidate that a neighbor wants to chat. The candidate should look reluctant to leave.

On a residential street, you need a larger team of four to six to cover more territory. Leapfrogging over vacant homes and talkative voters is still the key. If a team works together a lot, they can develop signals, such as the big loud "hello", to tell the rest of the team they have a live one at the door. The candidate can also wave over a canvasser and ask that she take down the concerns being expressed by the voter.

It's important not to walk too far up driveways or on lawns. Taking a big step back from the door gives the resident a little more space and comfort with a stranger at the door.

Identifying the vote and getting sign locations is a great by-product of candidate canvass. Some say the candidate touring the neighborhood is secondary to putting up signs and identifying the vote! Regardless, many people prefer to keep their political leanings secret, so it's best to approach this topic judiciously. After a bit of conversation about issues or with the candidate, you might say, "Have you decided how you're going to vote this time?" (Don't press it, but you'll get a large percentage who will tell you. Your voters are the ones to call to keep committed and drive to the polls on election day. With signs, you can just gently ask if they'd like one, but don't argue the point.

Door to door canvass should normally stop at 9:30 and there should be an issue de-brief at campaign headquarters. In one campaign, we were hearing at the door the perception that the candidate was weak on women's issues. We just flooded the neighborhood with female canvassers and didn't have to address this head on.

Speechwriters Play a Major Role in Communicating

But the Candidate Must Always Have the Last Word

Too many politicians aren't saying anything. There may be several reasons why. The biggest culprit may be focus groups which test phrases and themes. By definition, this type of research identifies the least objectionable, bland statement. Another factor is speechwriters who haven't worked for the candidate over a long period of time and aren't sure exactly what firm position s/he will take on an issue. So, the writer reverts to generalities and platitudes. This is also the refuge of a candidate who hasn't formulated a position yet.

Then, there are the venues in which politicians appear. Back-benchers in the parliamentary system may get to make bland statements for inclusion in "householders" mailed to constituents. A US Senator may drone on to an empty chamber.

The next column challenges politicians to take responsibility for the content of their speeches. They can still work with writers and media trainers, but taking ultimate responsibility will make for better content and performance.

Politicians should use the perks of office and campaigns sparingly—especially speechwriters. First time politicians should get into good speechwriting and delivery habits early in the game, and stick to them.

Having a speechwriter, even a great one, doesn't absolve the candidate from thinking. If your candidate has always wanted to sit in the back of a limo, rehearsing and editing a speech on the fly, nip this in the bud.

Candidates must take full responsibility for their own speeches. I've seen too many otherwise well-educated, powerful community leaders and executives dutifully receive, practice and read speeches that their writers prepare for them, without making any meaningful contribution themselves. Most candidates want a paragraph dropped or strengthened, but that's the kind of editing anyone can do. Excellent communicators take much more responsibility for their speeches than this rudimentary polishing.

One of my clients takes responsibility for the success of her speeches by writing her own text on 3 x 5 cards. She has several reasons for doing this. First, she is telling her story, with an appropriate level of ownership. Next, she actually saves time. How could any speechwriter know what personal anecdotes the speaker wants to use? In the time it takes to relate these personal stories to a writer, the speaker could put them on cards herself. Then, there's the issue of preferred style. Some speakers like cards, others full text, still others prefer key words. I've heard of one who likes a big grid on a piece of paper with key words and color coding in each square. Speakers may have different preferences for different topics or venues. There are so many variables that the speaker really needs to take ownership of them and simply can't delegate to a writer. My client practices her delivery as she's writing bullet points. She'll speak out loud, stand up and even deliver large portions of her speech to a mirror to see how much eye contact she can make with herself, and eventually her audience. In the time it would take to go over a draft with a writer, she has a finished and rehearsed product.

This methodology really paid off a couple of times. Once she was making an outdoor speech dedicating a statue. As she got up to the podium and put her cards down, a gust of wind blew her speech into the crowd. Rather than destroy the rapport with the audience, she stayed in the moment by joking that there were two things she could now do. One was to ask each audience member who had picked up a card to come up to the podium and deliver each card in their numbered order. The other is that she could deliver her speech from memory. She naturally opted for the latter.

She delivered a very credible speech from her own memory of having written and performed it. Can you imagine how lost a less authentic speaker would have been? If she had just read over the speech a few days before, she never would have had the confidence or knowledge to deliver it without the hard copy.

By the way, after dedicating the statue, audience members came up to congratulate my client on a great speech (and wave the 3 x 5 cards they'd collected). "I've got number 4". "I found number 6" they shouted in turn.

If I'm asked by a really good client to write a speech, I insist on delivering it orally. It is unproductive to watch a candidate or senior executive proofread my work. I arrange a time for me to deliver the speech orally, to show it is a workable product. Then I insist the client put his or her own personal touches on it for "ownership". This is a far more efficient system than passing countless drafts back and forth.

The wise use of a speechwriter starts with hiring someone who knows the candidate, the issues, great turns of phrases and has a wide and general education.

That last point is important. As the campaign unfolds, let alone governing, the candidate will have to speak about unforeseen issues. A campaign may begin with economic issues and end with education. The candidates' debate may focus on housing, but the week before the vote, health care may win you the election.

The relationship between the candidate and writer is important and should start with conversations about venues, themes, style and so on. There's little point in a writer shoving quotes from John Donne in a speech if the candidate has never heard of the 17th Century poet. I always believed Bobby Kennedy could quote ancient Greek poets from heart, but never thought George Bush "41" was a 'thousand points of light' kind of guy.

Next, how the speech is written, what size type, cards or paper and so on will be topics the writer and candidate must negotiate. I say negotiate because neither may be the best judge of what will work, but together they may create a winning formula.

Once the speech is written, it must be rehearsed, out loud, from beginning to end, without stopping. A candidate who fails to do this is like a person keyboarding madly and pressing Send—or

Print—without reading over his/her work. Or, it's like signing a contract without reading it over. The point to make with a reluctant candidate, is that s/he and the team spend a lot of time reading over and re-writing brochures and direct mail pieces. The candidate needs to treat the spoken word with even more care and attention. I tell candidates that just reading over a speech is proofreading and only pays $10 an hour.

The writer should then accompany the candidate to as many speaking engagements as possible. The writer and especially the candidate should watch video of these speeches and listen to audio tape. Audio tape can be used in planes, the car or gym. It allows the candidate to focus only on her voice—pacing, timing, volume, energy, intonation, breath control and so on. Most speakers need a lot more variety and energy. Candidates can watch a video tape with the volume off to focus on body language, energy and eye contact. Gestures should feel bigger and slower than in real life. Watching some of the tape on fast forward or fast reverse shows whether the gestures are symmetrical. The candidate should not look like a cartoon character, but the gestures should have a smooth rhythm to them. Naturally, the whole tape should be viewed at normal speed and volume as well.

Any candidate who resists rehearsal or reviewing tapes should be told to go look at the journalists covering the campaign. They rehearse their standup and questions before taping. They review their own and competitors' tapes. They have producers, make-up people, researchers and script assistants to make them look and sound better. I have asked candidates who are reluctant to rehearse what makes them think they can get good with less effort than professional communicators who have been successful for decades?

Style, Not Always Substance, the Key to Debate Victory

Attribution theory in the social sciences tells us that voters often make instant decisions on the credibility of a candidate. This decision might be based on the graphic look of brochures, clothing, semantic style in speeches, accent, hair, firmness of handshake and so on. In fact, studies show that 50–70 per cent of impact is based on body language—gait when walking, gestures, eye contact, facial expressions and so on. Can the term "image" sum up these matters?

Image is especially important in televised debates. Studies show that voters like to take in their candidates in one sitting. The debate is a chance to get the high points of the platform and the style of the candidate all in one night. The pressure is on to perform well on all indicators.

So, if it's image that gets a candidate elected, I'm all for it—whatever the term means.

About the most deceiving piece of conventional wisdom in the history of politics is that John F. Kennedy soundly beat Richard Nixon in the 1960 Presidential debate and this gave him the election.

First of all, that was the closest election to that point in history. One of the deciding factors was 120,000 stuffed ballots in Chicago.

Another was President Eisenhower not being able to remember anything his Vice President accomplished in eight years. When Kennedy and Nixon met after the election, the exchange between them is said to have been, "I'll guess we'll never know who really won". With an election that close, you just can't credit any one tactic or event with the win.

Secondly, most readers of *Winning Campaigns* are astute enough to know that voters who listened to the debate on radio thought Nixon won. The Vice President was mobbed at airports the next day and spontaneously kissed by young women.

But what even astute readers of this publication may not have done is to go back to the actual debates and study them. I have, at New York's Museum of Broadcasting, as part of a research project some years ago. I approached the debates with fresh eyes, because I am too young to have seen them live. I knew the conventional analysis of them, but tried to watch without bias.

The first thing that struck like a ton of bricks was that the debates were not at all a slam-dunk for Kennedy. I was very surprised at how nervous he looked. His eyes darted around. His hands shook as he made his signature pointing gesture for emphasis. His lips foamed up with spittle, and he occasionally spoke through thick moisture in his mouth. Kennedy also had a pronounced accent and the first of the blow-dried hair-dos. Months later, in his live news conferences, Kennedy wrote the book on grace, humor and efficacy under verbal fire. But that was later.

Nixon, for sure, was not telegenic. I saw him sweat. I saw him shifting from leg to leg because of a sore knee. He had a darker complexion and demeanor.

All things considered, Kennedy was probably the guy you might want to have in your living room for the next four years, provided he didn't spit on you. Nixon, would have been a humorless, earnest house guest, who would become tiresome quickly. But there was certainly no slam dunk.

That living room analogy is relevant in analyzing the Bush/Kerry and Cheney/Edwards debates. One of the most important questions voters ask themselves on debate night is, "Which one of these guys do I want hanging around my living room, in the TV set, for the next four years?" The President and Vice President become like house guests auditioning for a prolonged stay.

Why certain candidates pass this test and others fail is tough to describe. But I'll start with the intangible. There's something in radio and TV that's called "broadcast quality". It means that a particular recording or performance is up to a certain level of excellence. Home video cameras and cheap cassette recorders don't produce quality TV and radio. Neither do recordings made over the air, at a live concert, or from a TV speaker to cassette. Broadcast engineers have a hard time defining this quality, but it has to do with the equipment, mic placement, tape quality and other factors. You sure know it when you hear it.

There's also something that should be called broadcast performance–ready for prime time, perhaps. The intangibles here involve how a candidate "feels" to the viewer, not just how s/he looks. It's been called "star quality", "sparkle" and sometimes just plain "it". When you've got "it", everybody knows.

John Edwards is ready for prime time by a mile. Dick Cheney has something, but it sure ain't "it". Those are the two extremes. But Bush and Kerry are so close to the dividing line, it's sometimes hard to give a ruling as to which one is where.

Generally, Kerry is the better performer, with a soothing voice, open, powerful gestures, and an easy command of himself and the language. Bush is physically and syntactically awkward, grimacing, staring into the middle distance and coming up with garbled sound bites.

But here's where the analysis gets complex. Bush seems authentic. He's a real person, albeit a good ol' boy, warts and all. Kerry seems too studied, polished and purposeful. His gestures are text book correct, but so much so they appear unnatural. Bush's flaws add realism. If we were being criticized, we'd probably grimace like Bush, not smile like Kerry.

So much for the intangibles. There are also very concrete ways to judge how well a candidate will resonate with the electorate. The non-verbal clues include eye contact with the questioner or, when speaking to the electorate, with the camera lens. Leaning forward by two or three degrees, open, double hand gestures, pleasant facial expressions and smiling are all important.

Concrete verbal tools include using positive and avoiding negative words, lots of repetition and short sentences well under 18 words. My analysis shows Kerry using longer sentences than Bush. The speeches I and my researchers analyzed average 16.5 words for Bush and 18.6 for Kerry, so the average voter would understand Bush a little better. Bush is also using far more positive words—63 compared with his 6 negatives. Kerry used 22 positives and 27 negatives. A challenger has to be a little more negative since s/he's on the attack, but late in a campaign you have to get positive. Voters don't elect negatives.

Cheney lives up to his image, using 23 negatives and 51 positives in his speech—way too many negatives for an incumbent. His sentences are short—just 15.7 words on average. Edwards is using longer sentences—an average number of words of 17.1. He's using more positive words than negative, but at this late stage in the campaign, he still has too many negatives—40 in a recent speech versus 55 positives in the same address.

Like most debates, this year's had little new information, but were good "one-stop shopping" for candidates to meet the electorate. Knock out punches and huge gaffs are rare and few voters are swayed. But, votes solidify and the three to five day spin after the debate helps sway voters.

Even if readers of *Winning Campaigns* are preparing a candidate for a local, un-televised debate, the rule still is clear, simple, repeated, positive messages and positive body language.

CONVERGENCE

This piece on 'new media', or what I prefer to call fragmentation, began as a request to speak to about 150 military public affairs and other senior officers about circumventing the mainstream media. I made the speech in the summer of 2005. To put the research to good use, I reworked the thoughts in a political context and sent the following off to Winning Campaigns.

There's an expression in the political world called "hits". A hit is a connection with constituents—a speech, media appearance, newsletter and now blogs. Blogs can be a great way to achieve instant access and feedback. They can be a kind of cheap focus group to tell political leaders what's on the minds of constituents.

But they can also be a waste of time. Many are little-read, self-indulgent, rambling diaries, written by near-nuts who hope the mainstream media will pick up on their theories.

And the media does, in some cases.

But the real place to start understanding blogs and their potential in the political process is in taking a step back and understanding the broader issue of convergence. This involves understanding the technology people prefer to use to get their information.

In the 1960s TV show "Star Trek", Captain Kirk would flip open his hand held sensor/communicator and survey the planet he'd just landed on. Today, on this planet, I can open up my hand held device and take a picture or get the news. On vacation, I can dial a number and hear a walking tour of the neighborhood I'm in. If I'm car shopping, I can download information on a new car in a showroom that's closed for the weekend.

We are finally seeing a fundamental change in the way people send and receive information. I say finally, because this has been predicted for 60 years.

Flying cars, mail delivered by rockets and robots cleaning our homes just didn't materialize.

But technological convergence is actually happening. In 1968, Canadian journalist Patrick Watson wrote a book predicting that one day we'd come home, sit in an egg shaped chair and push buttons to see movies, shop or get the news.

Fast forward thirty-five years and phone companies are putting TV, piano lessons, nanny cameras and such on computer screens. The egg shaped chair isn't part of the deal though.

Whether campaigning or governing, a successful politician has to keep up with new technology. It is said that President Roosevelt and Winston Churchill wrote letters to each other during World War II. The information would have been four days out of date by the time the letter arrived. They also occasionally used the telephone—time zones and line quality permitting.

During John Kennedy's time, documentary maker Robert Drew invented a light weight camera with sound. If you haven't seen it, you can't imagine the difference between the coverage this afforded versus the static shot of stuffed shirts standing behind a microphone.

In the Vietnam war, reporters would talk a flight attendant into carrying a can of film to London or Hong Kong so it could get on the network news the next day. All those shocking reports from the war were at least 18 hours old.

But in those days 60 million Americans watched the network newscasts every night. Now it's dropped to 20 million, and their average age is 60.

The young demographic is getting its news from late night comedy and talk shows, the Internet (chat rooms, radio, blogs), MTV, satellite radio and cable.

Here are some facts and figures:

- Bloggers are young, wealthy and educated
- Blogging is publishing and therefore subject to all relevant laws
- Some companies encourage employee blogging as a way to reach out to customers
- Some companies fire employees for blogging about company information
- Blogs helped propel Howard Dean into national prominence
- Blogs helped destroy Dan Rather's career
- Some days 10,000 new blogs are created

But about 50 per cent of Americans have never even heard the word "blog". Only about 5 per cent of US companies use blogs and fewer are interactive. Even political blogs only attract about 5 per cent of Internet users.

Some say blogging has crested.

The first step in really understanding this fundamental change is to recognize that it's a change in form, not meaning. In the *Harvard Business Review,* business guru Michael E. Porter says "in our quest to see how the Internet is different, we have failed to see how the Internet is the same". Lawyers, businesses and politicians are having the same discussion about blogs as they had over a decade ago about email.

No one is entirely sure how any new technology will shake down, but look at it this way; the glass window in the car show room is a medium of communication. We look, become tantalized and buy. A TV set in an electronics store window broadcasting pictures of the car does the same thing through a different form of communication. Ditto the hand bill, barker on a soap box and even the WiFi (wireless hook up to computers) or VoIP (Voice Over Internet Protocol). These are all different ways of downloading similar information about that car.

The consumer doesn't care whether the pictures of the car are being broadcast over the air, arriving on cable, broadband (copper wire or fibre optic), VCR, CDRom (small or large), 8mm (16 or 35), Beta or WiFi. Consumers care about content—the car.

The important thing for a politician to address is fragmentation, not new technology. Constituents are still watching a screen—computer, TV, cell or Blackberry. The issue is control. If you wanted the news 30 years ago you watched the networks. Today there are a dozen choices and the consumer controls which to use. Cumbersome technology like "hot type" empowers elites. Simple technology like transistor radios or interactive Blackberry blogs empower users. This is almost as important as content.

The issue is also immediacy. In the old days, if you were angry at a newspaper column, you had to drag out a typewriter, bang out a reasoned response and pop it in the mail. Then email meant you could skip a few steps and get your message out quicker. Now blogs feature both instant access and the possibility of instant response.

Cyber-democrats can now say they "put it on their blog" or "told off a blogger". This may feel satisfying, but what if only one person reads it? How is it fundamentally different than sending a telegram forty years ago?

The trouble with technology is that there's no free lunch. You may gain immediacy and interactivity with the web, but you may also lose permanency and power. You may get high status with a *New York Times* piece, but you miss the MTV crowd.

But with a blog, a piece in the *Times*, or an appearance on a cable show that only two percent of the population watches, you can get a bounce or multiplier effect. Mainstream networks and cable news shows are reading blogs on the air to viewers, thus giving them legs. The *Times* piece can be scanned and emailed to thousands who would never otherwise read that newspaper. And just because Larry King only gets single digit ratings in most markets doesn't mean he isn't highly influential among other media and decision makers.

All media try to extend their brands into other media, gobble up existing media content, or want to be gobbled up. Historically, newspapers gobbled up handbills and signs by putting advertising on their front pages. They also ate up political pamphlets by providing commentary, coverage and advocacy. Early radio newscasts were written by newspaper journalists. TV gobbled up film, radio hosts and wire service reporters. Now, everybody's trying to put music, entertainment and news on a computer screen or a hand held device.

The trouble is the old media won't go away. Sure, we don't use hand-held megaphones much anymore. The Victorian stereopticon with two pictures that simulated depth when the wooden device was held up to the eyes morphed into View-Masters and then all but disappeared. But, for the most part, a new medium of communication doesn't replace old ones. They are just added on to the mix and overlap a little with the others.

It is not clear how convergence is going to work out. One good guess is that we will all have an information appliance to carry around which acts like a phone, computer, TV, stereo, movie theatre and newspaper all at the same time. But we're still going to have all those older media as well.

Politicians who need to connect with constituents, need to surf on the new media, while not ignoring the old.

CHURCHILL

This was written on my second visit to the Cabinet War Rooms in London, England. All political junkies are fascinated with Churchill, and I'm no exception.

To be a good surfer, you have to have a good wave. Good waves depend on the weather. Put another way, in politics, it's all "time and chance" as said in Ecclesiastes. The Biblical quote has been used by at least two heads of government for their biographies— President Jimmy Carter and Canada's first (and short-lived) female Prime Minister, Kim Campbell.

Logic would have dictated that George Washington, having lost most of the battles in the revolutionary war, would not have made a good political candidate. Right? Lincoln, having been rebuffed many times by the electorate, and having only limited militia experience, would not have been a good bet for a wartime commander in chief. Right? U.S. Grant, the magnificently successful and adored wartime general, would have made a great peacetime President. Right? Nixon was washed up in 1962 and Reagan was too old in 1980. Right?

Conservative thinker and writer William F. Buckley was once asked by "Tonight Show" host Johnny Carson who would win the next US election. Buckley indicated that if one gazed back to 1942 and saw who pundits knew would be the victors, one had a 70 per cent chance of being wrong. Time, chance, crying in New Hampshire, electroshock therapy and even assassination, play unexpected roles in the outcomes.

A mandatory pilgrimage for those interested in time, chance and politics is the fabulous museum dedicated to understanding Winston Churchill in London, England. I'm just back from my second tour of this much expanded attraction. To study Churchill in multi-media, a visitor must also tour the Cabinet War Rooms—the underground bunker used by the war cabinet to shield them from the Nazi blitz.

All politicians, and those who wish they were, should study the Churchillian context. He began his career on a horse with a saber and ended it with soldiers in space and nuclear weapons. He held high elected or appointed office from 1905 to 1965—unheard of in this era when media and electoral scrutiny chews up political figures in a few years. He fought in the Boer War, was captured and made a miraculous escape, commanded forces in World War I, helped invent the European Union and British Petroleum, and saved the world from totalitarianism—just to name a few accomplishments.

But on the other side, he has a few shortcomings. He was on the wrong side of the movement for Indian self-determination, denounced as a media-grandstander long before radio and TV, blamed for WWI's Dardanelles campaign (Gallipoli) and considered washed up long before WW II. In fact, in the late 1930s, visitors to his private club in London were warned to avoid the old man for fear he'd lock them in a rambling discussion of war, rumors of war and other intrigue.

And, although Teddy Roosevelt, John Connolly and Ronald Reagan managed to switch parties or create their own, none hold a candle to Winnie. He started out as a Conservative, then spent twenty years as a Liberal, and, after inventing a couple of parties returned to the Conservative fold. Even Sir Winston said something to the effect that anyone can "rat", but it really takes something to "re-rat".

Any politician who feels the electorate is ungrateful for the Herculean efforts the elected official must go to, should consider the tenuous hold Churchill had on power, even during his war years. In addition to fighting Nazis, keeping the Allies together and cajoling the US into the war effort, he had his own Cabinet and caucus to fight. Moreover, once the war was over, the electorate promptly threw the Great Man out of office.

The Churchill museum allowed me to read early public opinion surveys, explaining why voters turfed Winnie out. The reasons were as partisan and vitriolic as anything said about Presidents Nixon, Reagan, Clinton or Bush in a much more polarized era. Electors, right after Winnie won the war, said he was too old, out of it and over the hill. They criticized the party for trotting out the old warrior, and even referenced his excessive drinking.

Modern politicians who want a little benefit of the doubt from electors should consider what they are really entitled to in light of Churchill's getting relatively nothing.

But, for those who value monetary rewards, Churchill did make a fortune—first, as a war correspondent, attaching himself to regiments and operations in interesting parts of the world, and later as a journalist selling stories and books to the highest bidder. Decades ago, he received advances that current authors would kill for. He also did a favorable deal with the British Government for his country estate—none of which might pass ethics and media watchdogs today.

So, on the leadership and electoral success front, Churchill might not be an applicable model for modern day politicians, unless they're sure a Hitler-type character and a World War is waiting in the wings.

On the oratorical front, the conventional wisdom is that Churchill was a great speaker. I won't waste ink debating that point. But I will put the notion in context, for young politicians looking for a role model. Early in his career, young Winston memorized his House of Commons speeches. One day he went blank, stopped speaking, and had to sit down in silence and mortification. None of his wartime House of Commons speeches was recorded or broadcast. He'd make the speech and then edit, rehearse and record it for future broadcast. He'd polish and re-record until he was content with the outcome. We'll never really know what his real wartime speeches sounded like, because there's no authentic record of them. What we do know is that a post-war album of his speeches bombed because they lacked the drama that real wartime provided. There's that pesky time and chance again.

Then there's the controversy about whether an actor performed some of Churchill wartime speeches. The museum says no, but the voices I heard are so different, I find this hard to believe.

As I write this, sipping British Airways champagne on a flight back to North America, I'm also reminded of Churchill's wit. On his drinking, he once said he'd taken far more out of alcohol than alcohol had ever taken out of him. At a cocktail party, a woman once said that if she were married to him, she'd feed him poison. He retorted that if he were married to her, he'd drink it! At a garden party a woman guest was bitten by a bee on her buttocks. A man volunteered to suck the poison out of the affected area. Later, the man wrote to Winston asking if he remembered the incident. Winston said, not only did he remember, but he could think of little else since.

Modern politicians should make their geographic, rhetorical and ideological pilgrimage to the Churchill Museum in London.

Diplomats

This column deals with the timeless issue of how to have good relations with the media. Its theme is simple—it's a labor intensive business—based on human contact. I didn't realize until recently that my criticism of planning echoes business professor Henry Mintzberg's, for which he should get full credit.

For years I have been a sponsor of a dinner honoring diplomats. Several hundred interesting people show up including some former heads of state, many ambassadors and countless diplomats from the trenches.

One year this dinner provided an important lesson in networking and media relations that politicians and staffers need to know.

I love diplomats. They're well read, have been posted to half a dozen exotic locations and can pretend to be fascinated at a boring party at the drop of a hat. Politicians can learn a lot from diplomats.

I love diplomats because I've worked with them all over the world. I'm grateful for the unique experiences I gained during Hong Kong's handover to China in 1997, Europe '92, UN Conferences in Rio, Beijing, Vienna and elsewhere and even on less sexy issues like overfishing, our obligations under the Rio treaty, and rulings of the International Joint Commission.

A lot of the work I do for politicians and diplomats involves media relations. They want better relations, no relations and more positive relations at different times in their careers.

Among my most important lessons are that media relations is a labor intensive business. As soon as you make some contacts in the newspaper, all the players change when they go to a tabloid format. Your radio station contacts disappear when they buy a syndication service and downsize the newsroom to one kid from the community college. That reporter you've befriended at the TV station moves to a bigger market to do the weather.

It's a crazy business, but you have to keep plugging away.

One year I took my wife to this diplomatic dinner. She's been a public radio host, anchor and interviewer for decades. The presenter at the awards dinner was naturally going to acknowledge me as a sponsor, but also had the presence of mind to realize I was with my wife and take note of her occupation. Perhaps she asked around or had been a regular listener. Perhaps I'm just known as "spouse of...". I'm not sure. But this kind of attention to detail is what separates the children from the grown-ups at networking events.

At any rate, the presenter kindly referenced me and then went on to say, "...and Allan is here with his wife, Lorna Jackson, host of the network show "The World This Weekend". You may have also heard her on "As It Happens", "The Food Show" and many other programs over the years".

Other than the rabid talk show hosts, radio people are "shy-extroverts". Lorna blushed, but was happy to be known.

We ate our dinner, applauded the young diplomats who were being honored and started mingling and shuffling out when the event was over.

What absolutely amazed me was that in a room of several hundred people, many of whom have communication responsibilities for important trade and diplomatic files, not one single person walked up to meet Lorna. In the room were also political staff, several current and former cabinet ministers, senior civil servants and public affairs people.

Surely not everyone was too shy. Surely not everyone had baby-sitter problems. This was an opportunity to make a connection with someone responsible for two, half-hour news and public affairs broadcasts in prime time every weekend. The weekend is often a slow time, so Lorna's program involves interviews in addition to straight news. It's often hard to get a good source on the weekend, so having off hour numbers can be a godsend.

After wracking my brain as to why no one showed any initiative that day, I've finally come to a conclusion. Media guru Marshall McLuhan said that media often turn in on themselves to become their opposites. Like most of his impenetrable aphorisms, you have to think about this one. The automobile started out as an instrument of freedom and mobility. Now, it's a cage that traps its victims for hours a day in bumper to bumper hell.

The communications plan that started out as a means of letting senior management know what was going on, assigning tasks and measuring success has become an end in itself. I once wrote a line for a magazine stating, "planning is not actually doing anything, it's just planning to do something". An editor deleted it for fear of offending planners.

No doubt the government, the diplomats and the political staff all have communications plans. They involve buying time on paid wire services, holding formal press briefings, issuing news releases and so on. In fact, I happen to know one government department issues 600 news releases a year.

But none of this involves any human contact. The communications planning function has actually put more distance between news maker and journalist. Next time you're at a party and spot a journalist across the room, walk over and start a conversation. It might pay dividends on some slow news day in the future.

NETWORKING

*From both a democratic and practical perspective,
it's important to bring new people into the system.
I'm always amazed at how political and diplomatic
networking events feature the usual suspects.*

After doing work on the North American Free Trade Agreement,
I became friendly with Canada's Chief Negotiator, John Weekes.
John was a career diplomat who is now a private sector trade
advisor in Geneva.

He rose to be the top Canadian diplomat in charge of Canada-US
relations—the Senior Assistant Deputy Minister. During this assignment in Ottawa, I once remarked to John and his wife that they
must be out five nights a week at Embassy functions. They were
not, they assured me. I expressed amazement.

"Surely the Mexicans and the Americans, at the least, invite you
to their functions because of the trade deal". This was not the case,
I was told.

"What about the South Americans who want a similar deal, or
Israel that did get such a deal? Surely they want to pump you for
how NAFTA worked". The answer was again, "No".

"But now that you're the senior diplomat in charge of US relations,
surely the Americans invite you in that capacity to talk about a
variety of non-trade issues?" I was wrong again.

"But these diplomatic parties every night are a cliché. They exist.
Who's going to them if it's not you?"

John then gave me his theory.

"They're inviting each other" is how he began.

Over the years, John observed how diplomatic parties in world capitals featured mainly diplomats, politicians, traveling dignitaries and others from everywhere other than that world capital. So, in London, you might attend a party given at the French Embassy featuring Rhone Valley wine makers who had just won medals at a competition. In attendance might be the Dutch, Swiss, and South African Ambassadors, and the Australian High Commission staff. Some exporters, manufacturers and politicians would round out the guest list. They'd all mingle and mix.

The futility of this kind of event came up one time when I was advising clients in Japan. One ambassador told me he had no interest in going to an event at the Norwegian embassy where he would meet Africans. His country had an Embassy in Norway and embassies all over Africa. He figured that those posts were doing their jobs just fine, and he'd focus on meeting Japanese people while in Japan. He told me that's why the taxpayers of his country sent him to Japan, and he was content to fulfill his part of the bargain.

So, at diplomatic and political events, in world capitals or back home with constituents, several rules apply. These rules apply to the staffers, politicians and diplomats equally.

Don't talk to each other. If you're attending an event, it's to make contacts, work the room or work an issue—not talk to each other.

Expand the invitation list. Reach out to new contacts in business, government, academia and Non-Governmental Organizations. Bring in spouses and journalists. Reach out to up-and-coming high tech young people who will eventually blossom into important contacts for you.

Think strategically. Practice time management. In an event with 100 people, examine the guest list in advance and decide who you must see. Spend only five minutes with these people, with the goal of making enough of an impression that they'll take a call or a meeting later. Later is the time to do serious business. Then spend two minutes each with a dozen or so others. That's all the time you'll have. Be alert for surprise targets of opportunity, but when you've achieved your goals, get out. Few things destroy your reputation as a mover and shaker more than lingering at an event. You have a home to go to!

Arrive early. There's no such thing as being fashionably late for work. Register first and get a look at the guest list. Position yourself at the entrance and greet people as they arrive. The vast majority of guests are nervous and vulnerable at the moment of arrival. They'll be happy to have a friendly face to chat with. (Don't forget your friendly face).

Don't be shy. My wife says I'm not quite as witty and charming as I think I am, but then who is? My opening lines include, "What do you do in real life when you're not at political fundraisers?" or "What's your story?" You have to be careful about being too familiar, but in a room of 100 people, there's no time to be a wallflower. It's not the grade nine sock hop—get on with it.

Develop your story. "Hi, I'm a broken down ex-journalist, former political hack, turned academic spin doctor. How about you?" Seriously, you have just a few seconds to establish contact, so you better rehearse.

These days my best line is, "I'm a columnist for the prestigious magazine *Winning Campaigns*, and I bet my readers would be fascinated to hear about your work on the sub-committee".

I suspect you'll develop your own lines and style that are much better, but the net result should be more productive networking at events.

Julius Caesar

I am fortunate to live a short drive from three of the best theatre venues in the world. The Stratford Festival and the Shaw Festival are about an hour and a half away. Both have expanded their repertoire beyond Shakespeare and Shaw. Broadway is one and a half hours away by plane or an eight hour drive—a trip I make up to six times per year.

When I was a student at the UK's Leicester University, I had regular opportunities to stop in to London's West End for a few days on either end of the train trip about 100 miles north of the city.

It's been said that drama (and poetry) are just real life with the boring bits edited out. That's one of the reasons I also take note of the techniques I see on the stage. The playwright has worked hard to make those edits, and the actor is working hard to hold the audience's attention. The actor also wants to motivate the audience to applaud at the end. Isn't that just what speechwriters, politicians and policy makers do?

Politicians are used to repeating themselves. In fact, they often get robotic when delivering the same stump speech three times a day during a campaign.

But candidates have to learn to love repetition and sound fresh each time.

Learning to love repetition is one of the hardest lessons for modern politicians who see and hear their own remarks several times a day on TV, in newspapers and on radio newscasts. But they forget that effective oral communication requires repetition and even tautology for emphasis.

The master of repetition for clarity was never a candidate, but has been a successful playwright for more than 400 years—William Shakespeare.

Necessity was Shakespeare's motivation. He had to make a living with words. But he had a tougher task than most modern politicians. His audience had an average vocabulary of 3,000 words. Shakespeare was way above that—some say he had 27,000 different words in his writing. He also invented many words, and used some only once. His plays often ran for just a few short weeks and his words were spoken by actors of diverse skill.

At least modern candidates have an audience with about the same vocabulary, perhaps 18,000 words, and basic understanding of the topic—schools, taxes, terrorism and so on.

Shakespeare's other problem was the venue. Politicians complain about conference calls with reporters where they can't see the questioner, TV double ender interviews where they have to look into the lens of a camera, and board of trade meeting rooms with sullen looking audiences. Some even have to put up with hecklers. But those challenges are nothing compared with what the Bard and his actors put up with.

His old Globe Theatre could hold about 3,000 people—750 standing in the pit. Those 750 had to look slightly up at the stage while the rest of the crowd drank beer, picked pockets, argued with hookers and even had knife fights. Others sat on hard wooden benches and had their arguments up there. The chaos of a modern hockey rink is similar.

In Shakespeare's time, there was obviously no electricity and no curtain. So, there were no lights to dim or other signals that the play was starting. Two actors just walked out on stage and started talking. Most of what was said in the first few minutes of a Shakespeare play was not heard, seen or understood.

Then, during the play, patrons would shout out their views of the situation—"Don't drink the poison Juliet!" A rich patron sitting right on the stage might draw a sword and start to help in a fight scene too.

Shakespeare's solution to this madness was repetition. For example, in the first act of *Hamlet* he has actors say that the action is taking place at night more than a dozen times ("give you good *night*...has this thing appeared again *tonight*," etc.). Then they tell us indirectly that it's night another dozen or so times, talking about how cold it is or the fact there's a star in the sky. The first Act is only about 8 minutes long, and the fact that it's night is mentioned every 15 seconds or so.

Shakespeare achieved several objectives with his writing style, as a modern politician can. In addition to creating darkness and dread in the opening scene of *Hamlet*, Shakespeare's rhetoric is also a persuasive device. Through repetition, we are persuaded that there is a ghost and that something must be done about it. Shakespeare's lines also create a pleasing auditory effect. This should be a goal of modern candidates too.

One of the most famous cases of repetition in a Shakespeare play is in Act III, Scene II of *Julius Caesar*. Brutus needs the attention of the crowd to talk about Caesar's assassination. He uses repetition, beginning with,

> *"Romans, countrymen, and lovers..."*

In Shakespeare's day the word "lovers" meant dear friends, and dear friends are also countrymen and Romans. Brutus then asks that the audience:

> *"hear me for my cause, and be silent".*

As Monty Python might say, "If you were silent you would hear him, wouldn't you then?"

A line later Brutus demands full attention again: "...awake your senses, that you may be the better judge". Senses that are asleep wouldn't be able to judge much, would they?

Brutus also wants the audience to know he is honorable, so says:

> *"...believe me for mine honor, and have respect to mine honor, that you may believe..".*

He asks for belief twice and mentions his honor twice for emphasis. If you read that line out loud, you'll see that it also sounds nice. Speakers should always audio or video tape a rehearsal to hear whether the language in their speech is pleasing to the ear. They will hear how emphatic repetition sounds as well.

Right after Brutus speaks in Julius Caesar, Antony famously calls for attention with repetition, in much the same way Brutus just did.
"Friends, Romans, countrymen, lend me your ears..."

He calls Caesar's ambition *"...a grievous fault;/ And grievously has Caesar answer'd it..."* In the next 18 lines Antony mentions this "ambition" six times—every eight seconds.

Repeating Brutus' reference to honor, Antony says "Brutus is an honorable man/ so are they all, all honorable men". Again, if you read that line aloud, you hear the pausing and poetry that all the "ahhh" sounds create.

The line "And Brutus is an honorable man" appears twice in just eight lines. Honor is mentioned about every eight seconds too, appearing five times in 19 lines.

Antony mentions twice again that Brutus and Cassius are honorable men, and has an ulterior motive with all this repetition. He's building suspense until he can finally arouse grief and anger in the crowd for Caesar, who has just been violently assassinated. He is also heaping this praise on the "honorable" killers to cause the crowd to question whether they are indeed men of honor. The repetition hollows out word, causing it to lose meaning. The comparison of the word honor to Brutus' actions causes the audience to question those actions.

Other examples of this repetition include Act V, Scene I of *A Midsummer Night's Dream* where Pyramus lets everyone know his fate by stabbing himself and stating *"Thus die I, thus, thus, thus/ Now am I dead..."* Just in case we missed it, four lines later he states, *"Now die, die, die, die, die"*. Shakespeare may have wanted the line played for a laugh, but it may also be that the actor is letting all audience members in the round Globe get their money's worth by delivering the line to all sections of the house.

When King Lear enters with dead Cordelia in his arms he begins, *"Howl, howl, howl!"*

In *Macbeth*, Macduff enters in Act II, Scene III yelling, *"O horror, horror, horror!"*

So, the next time a political speaker is tempted to edit out a repetitive phrase, the better part of valor may be to keep it, and even put another one in for emphasis. And then emphatically put in repetition, just to make the point again!

Staying on Track

I'm still grateful to the US State Department and its spokesperson, Nick Burns (now Undersecretary) for allowing me to see, first hand, how they run press briefings. I am constantly asked by politicians, bureaucrats and executives about how to implement a competent, safe system of briefing the press. Politicians want to know what matters they should refer to the bureaucrats. Bureaucrats want to know if they'll be stepping on the boss's toes.

Around the time of writing this column, Canada's Foreign Ministry was re-visiting the topic. I happened to have business in Washington, so agreed to look into the issue, close-up.

In the end the Ministry did not install their own briefing room. But shortly after, we became involved in Kosovo and the Department of National Defense cut a hole in a concrete wall in their building to create a secure briefing room in which their senior officers could speak with reporters. The Foreign Ministry suffered the indignity and inconvenience of trekking across town to another ministry to participate in the briefings.

I'm still a fan of regular press briefings. Politicians need to understand that there are countless

mundane issues that their officials can provide
background on, while the Cabinet officer can pick
and choose high-road issues to speak about.
Officials need to understand that daily briefings can
be done safely, with proper research and rehearsal.

If a politician is not willing to rehearse performances fully, s/he should get into another business. No exceptions.

Rehearsal starts with research into the issues, full performances out loud in front of staff, and video taping of actual events for later analysis. If you think video taping every media interview, debate, speech and committee appearance is over the top, consider that there are few if any boxers, football players or other athletes who don't use game tapes. If the average pug has the sense to watch tapes, politicians need to exhibit twice the brains in their professions.

I've heard from someone who should know that The Great Communicator, Ronald Reagan, took media training in his last two weeks in The White House. This was after countless rehearsal and training sessions during two successful terms.

Pierre Salinger, John F. Kennedy's press secretary, tells the story of preparing the President for live, televised news conferences. They'd have a meal and Salinger would ask the questions he thought the reporters would ask. Kennedy would provide a full response to tricky questions.

I know politicians today are almost constantly beside themselves over the media. Political staffers pour over clipping files, rehearse the boss, issue press releases and stage events. One false step and the boss is toast and the staffer's looking for work at an agency.

I'm not sure it's all that hard to stay safe in front of the media. I often think of the toughest media spokesperson jobs in the world— The White House, The State Department and The Pentagon. You don't often hear of those spokespeople getting fired for saying imprudent or incorrect things.

It's no secret how these spokespeople stay safe. It's called "work". The Brookings Institution has documented how researchers begin their days early by seeing what stories are in the newspapers and which are developing on morning radio and TV newscasts. The researchers start framing positions on the issues of the day. The researchers for The White House, State and The Pentagon compare notes to make sure they'll all be on the same page. The spokespeople rehearse, and then it's show time!

The State Department's noon news briefing is not at noon, it's not news and it's not brief. It's held after 1:00 and there are a couple of rules that would give politicians a fright. First, there is absolutely no time limit. The event ends when a reporter shouts "Thank you". The politician who relies on a staffer to end the news conference, or say there's only time for one more question might panic at this rule.

Second, the spokesperson is not allowed to raise a topic or make any statement, but only respond to questions. Imagine a politician not being allowed to set the tone for a committee appearance or press briefing?

Third, the spokesperson, by convention, does not read any text. Imagine the politician without the crutch of a carefully crafted, polished and re-written text?

I've seen this first hand. It's a sight to see. Some years ago I was a guest at The State Department. Nick Burns, later Ambassador Burns, was the official spokesperson. Mr. Burns, like so many diplomats, is a real class act. He greeted me in the hall warmly, as if meeting me were a big event in his life. He even apologized for interrupting our conversation so he could go do the briefing.

The room is smaller than it looks on TV. But the world's press is there and the networks can put the feed live on air anytime they want. I sat in the back near the CNN camera, ready to watch the show. Mr. Burns' first order of business was to introduce me to the world's press! I couldn't believe I was hearing him from that famous podium with "The State Department" logo behind him say, "Allan Bonner is a media consultant who is here studying government-press relations and I hope you will welcome him". Two or three reporters looked around the room with that marvelous disdainful look reporters get when nobody important is introduced.

Then Mr. Burns got down to work. He began fielding questions, one after another. There were occasional follow-ups, as reporters tried to trap him into an imprudent response. He didn't bite. He regularly and professionally indicated he'd been clear before, had offered all the facts available and had nothing to add.

Very occasionally, he'd look at a thin, three-ring binder of notes he'd brought into the room. He'd flip a tab and indicate he had a statistic, the spelling of a foreign name or a fact to cite. But other than that, the whole show featured eye contact, upright posture and no notes.

At the end, after being thanked by the press, Mr. Burns and I went down the hall to his office. He apologized that he couldn't spend more time with me, but I understood that he had a major role in running the free world, so I quite understood.

Nick Burns had a much tougher job as State Department spokesperson than most politicians do. His "beat" was the entire world. He, his predecessors and successors have to answer questions about human rights in South Africa, Rwanda, European Union, terrorism, China's economy and agriculture in Argentina. I notice I do not hear of these spokespeople getting into hot water for saying the wrong thing or not knowing their facts.

The lesson is clear. There's no substitute for hard work. Sure staffers, researchers and outside consultants can help out, but ultimately, the individual politician has to take responsibility for what s/he says. Really reading documents provided, rehearsing out loud, taping speeches and committee hearings, playing back the tapes and making a commitment to continuous improvement is a cost of success in politics.

Specifics

I would love to see the play Democracy *again.*
I think my recent trip to Berlin might cause me to
appreciate Willy Brandt more. The delicate role he
played in détente, the dangerous clash of ideology
in walled and blockaded Berlin, and the Stasi
(secret police of East Germany) mole in Brandt's
office might be more compelling now.

However, I'm still adamant that intoning slogans
from balconies is not stirring political discourse.

In the Broadway play *Democracy*, by Michael Frayn, the main
character is the fascinating West German politician Willy Brandt.
He was the much loved mayor of Berlin, then Chancellor during
the cold war, and played a pivotal role in German unification.

I should have loved the play. I loved Frayn's British music
hall farce, *Noises Off*, and his intellectual offering from the other
end of the spectrum, *Copenhagen*. *Copenhagen* was a hit in New
York, and an even better production in my home city of Toronto.

Democracy should appeal to all political junkies. I even started
the night with the obligatory dinner at the landmark Sardi's
restaurant. But the play didn't work for me. The spy intrigue
was not intriguing enough. Why Willy was so beloved was not
entirely clear. His work on treaties and meetings in the East
have lost their meaning in the intervening decades. (Imagine a
play about Nixon's trip to China, or Eisenhower's worry about
inflation and the military industrial complex).

For a lot of history, "you had to be there".

A lot of policy, treaty making and lawmaking just doesn't stay exciting for years. But a politician's speech should live for a long, long time.

In *Democracy*, the Willy Brandt character is occasionally seen on a high balcony intoning the words "Have the courage to show compassion". There are cheers to show how beloved Willy is. But as I write this, I'm not sure I have the quote correct. He could have said "Have the compassion to show courage". For that matter, he might have been as well off saying, "Have the compassion to avoid courage," or vice versa.

The point I wish to make about political speeches is that they must be specific to the candidate, the times, the party and the audience. Otherwise, you're just so much background music and wallpaper.

Take the candidate, for starters. Each politician has to decide whether s/he wants to be a lobbyist or a legislator. A lobbyist can do a lot of good public service through part time agitation and annoying of elected officials. If a person thinks s/he has a better idea of how to implement the laws of the land, then lobbying is an honorable and productive profession.

But there comes a time when a political person honestly feels that the existing laws are not serving society well. If s/he also believes that current elected officials are not predisposed to passing new and more proper laws, s/he should decide to become a legislator. So, when this candidate makes a speech, s/he should be distinct from other candidates. No other candidate should be able to make most of that speech and get away with it.

The speech should also locate the candidate in the times in which we are living. When I analyze political speeches for clients, I read a lot of platitudes and flag waving. Words about duty, patriotism, honor, sacrifice and so on are peppered through many speeches. Every age is concerned about jobs, productivity, competitiveness, trade, education, welfare, dignity and such. But what are the specific hopes, aspirations and needs of this generation, right now? What are the specific solutions that suit these times? Most speeches miss this specificity.

Similar to my rule about whether a candidate should be a lobbyist or legislator, the candidate needs to choose a party, and even a wing of a party, wisely. If a candidate has a policy that s/he thinks any wing of any party might implement, then it's not a very specific ideological position. The reason to get into politics is that *the powers that be* will not do what you think is right, in the way you think is most efficient. If you can articulate this, you have what Madison Avenue calls a "unique selling proposition", and you will be remembered. If your speech is full of platitudes, your message ends up being "me, too".

David Letterman had a regular feature on his show called "George W. Bush...Liar". After the intro to the bit, there's a clip of the President saying, "It's great to be back in (pause) Des Moines" (or wherever he is). To me, this signifies the difficulty of being authentically present with your audience. I'd start by asking the politician if it really is "great" to be back in this community or with this audience. If so, why is that? If you dig long and deep enough, you just might find that there's an historical event worth mentioning. Perhaps there's a business whose success illustrates a point about your approach to economics. Maybe a plant closure illustrates a point too. But there must be some good reason to be nattering on with these folks, especially if you flew all day to get there. My advice is to find out what those reasons are and capitalize on them.

The politician who just gets up and parrots generally-accepted values and principles, misses an opportunity to offer a concrete message. The candidate who sings the praises of the local organizer or entrepreneur without getting specific is condescending and wasting everybody's time. The local hero has a fascinating story and if s/he is worth mentioning, then it's worth doing the hard research to tell the whole story. It will be a real moment, creating a lasting link between audience and speaker. Moreover, the candidate just might learn a little about local issues, politics and people.

In short, the litmus test of a really good political speech is that it cannot be delivered by just anybody. It is custom-tailored for a particular candidate. The speech cannot be delivered in any community to any audience at any time.

The next time you proofread a speech, imagine if sections could have been delivered in the North, South, East or West. Would they have worked in a small town, as well as the big city? Can you hear three or four Presidents from both parties saying these words? Could you imagine the message working in your parents' time? If so, you've got boiler plate and blather. As they used to say in old time newspapers—"Get me re-write!"

Party Time at the US Consulate

I won't say where this networking event happened, but there's no excuse for an Embassy, High Commission, Commission or Consulate to conduct an event as unfocussed as the one I recount below.

There's no such thing as a casual event in politics. Every event in a politician's life means something—or should.

When I was invited to the retirement party for a prominent US diplomat, I thought I'd get a lesson on how things should be done. Diplomacy, like political networking, is the fine, painstaking art of subtly making others feel important and welcome, while achieving your objectives.

When I arrived at the backyard of the diplomat's official residence, the first person I encountered set a poor tone. The young staffer's opening line was something like, "Who are you?" I responded with my name.

"And where are you from?" the schmoozer asked.

I know this is a code phrase to find out why I was invited and what company I work with, but I find it so inept that I usually respond, "Toronto". (Sometimes I state, "Montreal" because I was born there).

The schmoozer/diplomat didn't have another question and didn't offer anything interesting about his own work, so I moved on. As a general rule, if you can't say something that interests an ex-journalist, you're not a very interesting person.

The event was poorly attended, not quite filling up the mid-size backyard. Canadian media guru, Marshall McLuhan famously said, "The medium is the message". When the medium is a half-empty backyard, that sends a clear message about how important the person and the event are.

Worse, nobody capitalized on the people who did show up. The most obvious case involved the newly elected mayor. He'd campaigned on a controversial ticket involving transportation policy that was to have a profound effect on trade and the movement of people in and out of the city.

But, you'd think he was part of the catering staff, walking around alone. If I'd been him, still high from victory, I'd have thought these diplomats were purposefully snubbing me. Silence is also a profound message.

Here's what should have happened. A small team of staffers should have met a few times long before the event to construct a comprehensive guest list. They should have brought in a few outside volunteers from the university, local politics and journalism for advice.

In a city of a couple of million, there would be a couple of dozen professors, journalists and business leaders to invite. Part time professors, occasional columnists and young entrepreneurs who work from home should not be ignored. Neither should the multicultural community. A proper and complete list is not going to jump up and bite the organizers, nor can it be bought from media companies, list brokers, or the Board of Trade. Lists go out of date two per cent per month and journalists, for example, are notorious nomads. Organizers need to augment bought lists with their own work on the phone.

This phone research will pay huge dividends. You'll find the retired journalist who writes the odd editorial with no by-line and acts as a mentor for younger staff. You'll discover the professor who is just starting to research an important public policy matter. You might even figure out how to find the computer hippies working in their parents' basements.

Once that list is done and the invitations mocked up, two words should be added—"and spouse". There are more women in professional schools than men, and the workforce has been about 50 per cent female for decades. Yet I am astounded that spouses are usually considered female and are ignored. With a guest list of 100, there's a very good chance that a dozen or more spouses will be contacts that you had been hoping to make. Spouses are in industry, journalism, polling, academia and every other nook and cranny of the community you're trying to reach.

At the event, the first rule is no eating on the job. Canadian diplomat Colin Robertson, in charge of such matters in Washington, says he has a sandwich in the kitchen before the event and only pushes a few bits of food around on his plate at sit down dinners. He wouldn't be caught dead with a drink in one hand and a samosa in the other—he's working, which involves shaking hands and talking. Mouths and hands should be full only of words, business cards and other hands, in that order.

The next rule is to develop a short pitch about who you are and what you do, before pumping the guest. Then ask an open ended question such as, "Tell me a bit about you and your work".

If you've studied the guest list properly, you should have a few targets you want to meet. So should other members of your team. This will allow you to drop little rejoinders about how you've heard of the guest's work, spouse's work, or read about her in the papers recently. Nothing is as flattering as showing your knowledge of the person.

Then you can ask if the journalist who's on the business ethics beat has met the professor doing research into such work, or the new VP Environment for the resource sector company who is also present. As you introduce guests to each other and to your fellow staffers, you're developing as deep a relationship as possible at a short party or fundraiser.

With any luck, about a dozen will be really grateful for the introductions and your data base will be growing and deepening.

As for a guest who is as big a target as the newly elected mayor, missing out on his presence is like missing an open net in hockey. As he's walking up the driveway, one staffer should attach himself like glue to the guy and introduce him to everyone present. The mayor will get the message you care about him and guests will be pleased to have met the new celebrity. Two or three of the introductions will pay off for one of the parties who will be doubly grateful in the future.

The payoffs will be invitations back to other events for you, your staff and your boss. If it's a fundraiser, the payoff is money. If it's a campaign kickoff, volunteers will be a result. After running two or three such events, your backyard and campaign will be known as the place to be.

HAMLET

This article is an example of getting multiple uses out of a piece. I've studied and seen the play Hamlet *for years. Among the best versions I've encountered are at the Stratford Festival, Ontario, (staring Richard Monette, who later became Artistic Director), and a version in Lithuanian!*

The Lithuanian version was part of an exchange of international companies, staged on Toronto's waterfront. The set was startling—ancient, rusting pieces of machinery. A giant buzz saw blade was hanging centre-stage, and dripping with water. Occasionally, an actor would lash out and beat the buzz-saw blade with a length of chain. Other pieces of machinery were wheeled in and out.

All this may sound distracting, but even in Lithuanian, Shakespeare has an auditory arc and a visual appeal.

At any rate, all my Hamlet *experiences have culminated into trying to learn a few communications lessons from the great play. The piece below has appeared in* The Globe and Mail *as advice for business speakers and in* Winning Campaigns *for candidates in elections.*

Political speakers perform best when they take a few moments before a major event to consider strategy. What's the purpose of the event? Will everyone be able to see and hear me? What tone is appropriate? Should I show emotion?

If a speaker is really lucky, s/he has a trusted coach or ally to give a bit of advice. Even luckier is the speaker who gets advice from one of the greatest playwrights in history.

Well, that's what happened in Shakespeare's play *Hamlet*, when the young Prince of Denmark gave a group of actors advice on how to work a room. He was getting the actors to help set a trap to expose his step-father, so he was serious about achieving a specific purpose—as political speakers should be. There was also a huge potential payoff for Hamlet—de-throning his uncle and perhaps getting the throne himself—just like in politics.

It's great advice and still fresh, 400 years after it was written. Hamlet's advice can be boiled down to a few, easy to remember categories:

Be Comfortable

An audience won't pay attention if they're uncomfortable. To get an audience comfortable, the speaker has to be at ease too.

Hamlet insists that speakers' words must be spoken easily, or "trippingly on the tongue". Too many politicians sound as if they're reading stone tablets, laboring, on each word. They must remember to speak directly to individual audience members, many of whom are just a few feet away. Even formal speeches should be conversational in vocabulary and tone. The speaker should look at ease with gestures, body language and eye contact. Looking at ease means being comfortable with the topic, having eye contact with individual audience members, using positive, reinforcing gestures, having a pleasant, resonating voice and not pacing or fidgeting.

Volume

Hamlet cautions speakers not to sound like "the town crier", shouting in the streets. Too many politicians mistake volume for intensity. Just because someone is shouting, doesn't mean s/he's emotionally involved, sincere, done homework or anything of the kind. Shouting is just shouting and does not take the place of research, sincerely held views, sound policy or rapport with an audience. A speaker must be heard, but should not "split the ears" of audience members.

The solution to the volume problem is to try sincere emotion or purpose instead of decibels. A confidential tone, loud whispering, intensity, energy, pausing, pacing, speed and variety all work better than volume, depending on the person, topic and room. The best thing to do is rehearse the speech, in the actual room and try out different techniques that don't involve volume. Also, have someone stand at the back of the room give honest feedback.

Gestures and Body Language

Hamlet warns speakers to "not saw the air too much with your hand". Gestures should be made "gently". In fact gestures should be larger than real life—you're hard to see from the back of a hotel ball room. Larger gestures allow the speaker to reach out and over a podium to the audience. But these gestures need to be slower than in real life, otherwise the speaker will look like s/he's spouting propellers and trying to take off. Hamlet warns that speakers are in danger of creating a "torrent, tempest, and ...whirlwind of ... passion". The antidote is "temperance...smoothness".

This means that active verbs work better than adjectives, specifics are mandatory and pounding a podium doesn't replace a well thought out policy. The power should be in the ideas. The speaker's body and voice will then be a natural delivery mechanism. Speakers who are light on content often try to pump things up with phony, puffed up gestures and rhetoric. Hamlet cautions this may make the "judicious grieve".

As a rule, bigger rooms need bigger gestures. Gestures deserve a full rehearsal on video, the same way a speech deserves to be practiced out loud before delivery. The video will show if gestures, volume and facial expressions are appropriate for the room, the topic and the audience.

On my last visit to Stratford, Ontario, I quizzed David Prosser, Director of Literary Services for the Shakespearean festival there. He says a key to the kind of naturalness and authenticity Hamlet is advocating is purpose and connection. Gestures should be for the purpose of supporting what the speaker is saying. A speaker in rehearsal must ask whether that shrug, grimace or hand gesture supports the text of the speech, and whether it comes naturally.

Mr. Prosser adds that one of the hardest things is to just stay still while being introduced, or when listening to a question. The key is concentrating on the moment, not your self-consciousness. This means clearing the mind, not thinking about hobbies or other business goals, but making that moment in the speech the most important and only mental focus.

Mr. Prosser adds that actors often make the mistake of playing emotions rather than objectives. The actor's objective is to get something accomplished—bury somebody, kick them out of the room or move the plot along. Playing the emotions often means too much focus on wild gestures, quivering voice or grimacing face. Playing the objectives will focus on the job at hand.

A politician may be outraged over a policy or elated because of a new piece of legislation. Outrage and elation may be good reasons to make a speech, but are not good content on their own. Solving problems and meeting constituent needs with specific initiatives is more likely to get the desired reaction from the audience.

Be Natural

But Hamlet also cautions performers not to be "too tame" but to use "discretion". If you are excited about a policy, say so, but also show it in your body language, gestures and facial expressions. "Suit the action to the word, the word to the action", is the most famous advice Hamlet gives. This means that sincere, bright eyes, outstretched hands with palms at a 45 degree angle, elbows at 90 degrees and leaning into the audience a little, say more than a page full of platitudes.

Achieving this balance can create a naturalness in the delivery and allow the speaker to hold a "mirror up to nature". We've all seen stuffed shirts at the Board of Trade lunch. Most audience members wonder, if this guy's such a big shot, and knows so much, why does he look so uncomfortable?

This naturalness applies to movement as well. From the back of the room, speakers look like little heads on sticks behind the podium. It's relaxing for them to walk, move, reach out and be seen. Phony, uncomfortable or egotistical speakers who have "strutted" on the stage have only "imitated humanity", according to Hamlet. Naturalness comes by thinking about and studying the content of the speech, and by practicing in front of a mirror, video camera or trusted advisors, so that body, speech, face and words are all in sync. Advisors and family members can spot discomfort, nervousness or lack of command of the material and must be frank with the speaker.

Ad-Libbing and Humor

Ad libbing can be dangerous, even for seasoned speakers. Both humor and off the cuff remarks can put an audience at ease, but are hard to do well. It's best to be very careful and stick to the script until a speaker is confident s/he can deviate effectively. That's one reason why Hamlet cautions to "speak no more than is set down".

There's always a danger of speakers delivering lines to make "themselves laugh". While this may also get a cheap laugh from the audience, the price often paid is the sacrifice of content. Hamlet says "some necessary question" in the content of the speech may be lost by the audience. Asides, jokes and witticisms must support the content of the speech or help an audience understand the speaker or issues better. Otherwise, Hamlet says, the speaker is "villainous".

We don't call boring or bombastic speakers "villainous" much anymore, but perhaps we should. Certainly politicians who have not read Hamlet's advice, picked up a few self-help books in the remainder bin, listened to family members, worked with trusted allies or used video-taped rehearsal are guilty on all counts.

Humor in Speeches

*This column actually had its origins many years
before I started writing columns. As speechwriter
and full-time Executive Assistant to Mayor Mel
Lastman, I always had a speech or two on the go
for him. One day, after he'd returned from a Florida
vacation, my boss handed me a joke book.*

*"Try working some of these into your speeches,"
he asked.*

*The trouble was that the Mayor was and is as
unique a character as New York's Ed Koch or
Chicago's Richard Daly. Generic jokes won't work
with such unique characters. Worse would be jokes
in which you can hear the rhythm or style of a
polished monologist such as Letterman, Leno,
Stewart, Maher or Miller.*

*So, I developed the simple approaches listed below
that can work with any boss. They can then be
refined as the speechwriter begins working more
regularly with the speaker, getting to know preferences and style.*

*This, too, has appeared in several publications,
including* The Globe and Mail.

Humor

It's normal to fear public speaking. But what's worse, is speakers going over the text just before the Board of Trade lunch and being bored with their own remarks. This turns healthy fear into panic. Some speakers want to inject a few jokes into speeches at the last minute—and that's dangerous.

Sure, humor puts audiences at ease. A chuckle relaxes the muscles. A smile creates bio-feedback so that a listener is smiling mentally as well. If you're smiling with a speaker, you're more alert and the memory and even physical experience with that person will be profoundly more positive.

But how to get that humor in the speech? Humor is a double-edged weapon. It can injure the user as much as the listener. One of the best tips from self-help books and the rubber chicken circuit is the three Rs of humor—real, relevant and rehearsal.

Safety and success start with being real.

Real

The first R for real should remind speakers to be realistic about what they're up against when they try to be funny.

The most successful comedians in the world break in new material with highly paid writers and endless editing. No business speaker is going to compare favorably to these dedicated professionals by just sprinkling a few jokes into the text.

Also, the audience for comedy events is primed. They've had drinks, are relaxed and hoping to be entertained.

No political audience is this ready to laugh, especially at amateur humor. Also, politicians often deal with sensitive topics, and if there's a wrong way to take a joke and put it on the front page of the paper, you can bet somebody will.

A realistic expectation is to generate a chuckle, or smile. Thunderous applause and gales of laughter are for TV shows and night clubs.

Candidates should start where the pros do, by gathering and testing new material on a weekly basis. Anecdotes, stories, news items and quotes can be thrown in a file for future use. Oddball research findings, legal rulings, incomprehensible government regulation and the deal that got away often have humor value.

Jokes about sex, gender or physical attributes? Get real! Male speakers over 45 must remember they look like old geezers to audience members under 30. Off-color remarks will be creepy. Remarks should be suitable for a teenage daughter or neighbor.

Novices should make one attempt at humor per speech until s/he has a repertoire of just three to five workable lines per speech.

If a line falls flat, keep going, don't re-tell it, explain it or remind the audience it was a joke. Just move on.

Relevant

An audience doesn't attend a speech primarily to be entertained. So the good news is that if there is a chuckle, the low expectation will mean the humor will be very well received. But the political audience wants to hear something relevant to the day, the issue or the situation they're in.

When US President Ronald Reagan debated Walter Mondale in the 1984 American election, he was 72 years old. His mental ability and stamina were issues. During the debate Reagan said, "I don't think age should be an issue in this campaign. I won't hold my opponent's youth and inexperience against him".

Concern was dismissed out of hand with gentle, relevant humor.

Bartlett's Quotations is a good place to start finding relevant material. So is the daily newspaper, industry magazines and quality business publications.

I was in a small audience at a Canada/US Business Association meeting in Niagara Falls when the late Senator Daniel Patrick Moynahan said he was reminded of a quote from Soviet dissident Alexander Solzhenitzyn who likened North America to a bottle of milk with Canada being the cream floating on top. There was tremendous applause from both the US and Canadian audience members. It was relevant to the audience which was focused on the trading relationship between the two countries.

Another litmus test is to ask yourself if audience members have dealt with the issue recently. Have they seen it in the news or will soon be encountering that law, regulation or challenge? If so, you have a relevant core to a humorous line.

If you think the line might work with five other audiences, any time in the past five years, don't use it.

Rehearsal

Winston Churchill said, "I need not recount the pain I had taken to prepare, nor the efforts I had made to hide the work of preparation". He is said to have spent hours practicing, which is a big part of why he's known as a great speaker.

But most business speakers spend very little of their business days speaking, and most of the time reading. That's why they rehearse a speech by skimming the words and mumbling to themselves. That's proofreading, not rehearsing.

Proper rehearsal is out loud, in full voice and with full gestures. It should be in front of a video camera, audio tape machine and trusted colleagues.

Most speakers spend their lives looking at themselves backwards in the mirror and hearing their voices through the bone and flesh of their own heads, not the air as audiences do. So, few speakers actually know what they look or sound like.

Video and audio playback of rehearsals gives the speaker vital self-knowledge. Business researcher Chris Argyris, writing in the *Harvard Business Review* says just "listening to the tape is an education in itself". It "slow[s] things down" for an executive who is tempted to "produce a new conversation in....milliseconds".

For humor, it's important to deliver the quote or story several times around the water cooler, to neighbors and to family members to see if it has the desired effect. Then, when it's told in a real speech, it will sound natural.

Professional actors put in their rehearsal time too. After a recent performance at the Shaw Festival in Niagara-on-the-Lake, Ontario, the actors stayed on stage to answer questions. It was a great opportunity to hear from the group that famed New York theatre critic John Simon has called "the best repertory theatre on the entire continent".

One audience member asked how much rehearsal is involved for a play. The actor said the rule is one hour for every minute on stage, plus extra time if there's singing, dancing or accents. The next time a business speaker balks at a run through of a speech, remember s/he's probably getting off easy by this calculation.

A Cultural Federal Bureaucrat, Bernie Ostry was One of a Kind

Not a politician, but entirely political, Bernie Ostry wrote about politicians, befriended them and advised them. I was lucky to have worked briefly for the quintessential mandarin and survived. The Hill Times *ran this and* The Globe and Mail *ran a shorter version the week of Bernie's death.*

If you didn't have a chance to work with Bernie Ostry, you have missed one of a kind. There won't be another like him in the civil service, so you better enjoy these reminiscences of mine.

I was in government relations at TVOntario in the 1980s. This is the time Bernie (how he introduced himself to me) slid over from Deputy Minister at Citizenship and Culture to Chair and CEO of the provincial educational broadcaster.

His reputation preceded him. Bernie the academic. Bernie the author. Bernie the cultured, profane, smooth talking street fighter.

I won't forget the gleam in his eyes that I could just see over the gold reading glasses he kept perched on his nose. He was very small physically, even frail, but he could intimidate with his intellect. He had a soft, powerful, silica-sand voice that commanded attention. But it is the slightly crooked finger that gently beat a tattoo on a spot about three inches from my chest that also still resonates.

Bernie the friend of Pierre Trudeau (same gleam, by the way). Bernie the inventor of Canadian multiculturalism (while an Ottawa mandarin). Bernie the natty dresser.

Shortly after Bernie arrived at TVOntario, we were due to go in front of the Ministerial "estimates" committee at the legislature. Opposition politicians were ready to grill the Minister, Deputies, and agency heads on big picture spending.

I'd prepared a briefing book for my new Chair and presented it. "Lookit…" (out came the finger) "The thing you need to tell me is the three things you want me to say to these guys, regardless of what they ask (pause). But, I'm not going anyway, because of the constitutional issue—you go".

Constitutional issue? Bernie had cooked up this notion that a former Deputy Minister could not be compelled to appear in front of a standing committee of a legislature if he'd just been Deputy of the Ministry under scrutiny.

Legal scholars will know this as the "Notwithstanding the invitation, Ostry doesn't want to go" clause.

Off I went, sitting with the Chairs of the Royal Ontario Museum, Ontario Science Centre, McMichael Canadian Collection, etc. I pulled it off.

Then there was the "Northern Ontario" advisory council meeting of TVOntario. Bernie got a government plane to take us up to Kirkland Lake where he gave the locals a lecture in geography. He'd been born North of this spot and most of Canada was North of this spot, etc., etc.

On that trip, our car got to the plane first. Bernie got in and told the pilot to take off—without my colleagues in the other car. As the propellers turned over, I grabbed the arm of Suzanne Grew-Ellis and, in a loud voice, started the Humphrey Bogart speech from Casablanca. "If you get on the plane, you'll regret it, maybe not today, but soon, and for the rest of your life".

This stalled for enough time that we didn't leave anyone behind. Bernie seemed to like my sense of the absurd.

But the best stories were ones I only heard about. Bernie ordering a bottle of champagne in a restaurant and giving the waiter hell for pouring a little for others at the table. Bernie getting a call from Conrad Black, bragging about his new toy—*London's Daily Telegraph*. Bernie having breakfast at the Park Plaza in Toronto and shouting over the room to a government official, "Where's my hundred grand?" (they were late on a funding check).

I once took a deputy minister on a tour of TVO. He asked what I did. I said I was in charge of government relations. After a pause I added, "It's kind of like being Pierre Trudeau's foreign minister—I don't do much of anything". He got it.

One of Bernie's first acts at TVO was to pry almost double the budget out of the province. (We weren't sure what to do with it, frankly). The other was to take a five year experiment in French language broadcasting and turn it into a full French network—TFO. We did it, but when Bernie tried to take credit for doing this, one mid-level provincial mandarin responded, "But, who asked you to?"

Then there was Sylvia. Mrs. Ostry was Deputy at Industry and Trade (writing an economics text on the side) while Bernie was being Bernie. In a later life in Ottawa, I'd bump into her, bum a smoke, and we'd chat. I told her Bernie stories and she'd laugh that throaty smoker's laugh of hers.

But I made her look off into the middle of the room when I told her how I coped with some of Bernie's lectures. I'd just look over to the framed glamour shot of Sylvia that Bernie kept on his desk. It was a real 1940s, Hollywood diva profile. Sylvia said she had no idea he even had it. It was a nice moment, and the only real favor I actually did for Bernie.

'Don't Make up Any New Words'

*Right out of grad school, I became executive assistant
to the longest serving mayor in the world. What an
education! I began to really find out how politicians
and governments work, and how to write something
other than news, quickly and accurately. But then
there was the issue of writing for the Mayor's particular style—and challenges. On his retirement, I wrote
this piece for* The Globe and Mail.

Twenty years ago, almost to the day, I started my term as Mel Lastman's executive assistant. Mel was mayor of North York at the time.

My first assignment was to brief the mayor on the Toronto Transit Commission's long-range plan. To show Mel that he had hired the right guy, I boiled all this down to four main bullet points on half a sheet of paper, which I proudly handed him, plus some background.

My new boss grabbed a cigar, lit it – puff, puff, puff – until a mushroom cloud formed around his head. Then his eyes grew wide and he looked at me as though I had just beamed into his office from the transporter room on Star Trek.

"Oh ... do you mind cigar smoke?"

"No," I said, and Mel interrogated, "What on earth does this mean?"

"Those are just the main points, Mr. Mayor. Just read them and then we can discuss the background and what to do".

Mel read. "I can't understand a word of this. It makes no sense. There's no logic to it," he said.

I knew I had to nip this in the bud. "Mr. Mayor," I said in my most authoritative voice, "you have to understand that I have to go through these documents in a logical order and come to some kind of logical conclusion".

The Mayor shot back: "That's fine, you do that. Just don't give it to me that way".

Then there was the speechwriting. Mel has confessed to a reading disability – dyslexia perhaps.

I once wrote for the Mayor: "I am appalled with recent developments..."

Mel read, "I am applauded ...".

He shouted at the desk between us: "Applauded, are you nuts? Who in his right mind would be in favor of this? Name one person!"

I explained that appalled means you're mad.

"Just say what you mean in these speeches. And don't make up any new words," was his sound advice.

Another time, I wrote that he was "acutely aware" of some problem or another. "Acute?" he asked. "This isn't a medical speech".

"Mr. Mayor," I explained, "acute just means you're very aware".

"No medical terms in any speeches. I'm not a doctor!"

I kept my job and sanity by learning to do a pretty good impression of the Mayor. I would run into his office wild-eyed, saying something like, "Mr. Mayor, this new metro transit plan is nuts!"

"Nuts?" the Mayor asked.

"It's the tail wagging the dog," I said. I explained how GO Transit riders from the suburbs could get a free transfer onto the Toronto Transit Commission system. The metaphor grabbed him.

"Write a press release saying how nuts this is. And why not put a headline on it like 'Tail Wags Dog' or something". Now that it was his idea, I was home free.

Once, I wrote a series of letters to other Ontario mayors. One turned out to be dead. Mel scrawled across the letter: "This man is ded— D.E.D. Do not send unless you are prepared to hand-deliver".

I left the mayor's office 18 years ago, but occasionally run into my old boss. Usually he'll look me in the eye, smile and say, "How are you," looking at my name tag, "Allan".

Last week, I met him in his Yonge and St. Clair neighborhood. I stuck out my hand and asked, "Do you remember me this time?"

The Mayor did, and even though these are his last days in office, it feels good to have finally secured a position in Mel Lastman's famous memory.

LUNCHES WITH WOLVES

I couldn't say no to lunch with Ambassador Taylor, even though I'd just eaten..

Not a politician, but perhaps Canada's most famous diplomat, Ken Taylor is the hero of the Iranian hostage taking incident. Circumstances made my lunch with Mr. Taylor one of those remarkable New York experiences you just don't forget.

I've had other encounters since, but this one was worth writing up for The National Post.

Having a power lunch in New York City is always exhilarating. But I once had two such lunches, back to back, on the same day. And one was with revered diplomat Ken Taylor, hero of the so-called "Canadian caper," when he hid American diplomats during the Iranian revolution and smuggled them out of harm's way.

I asked the Ambassador if he'd mind a late lunch–about one o'clock–since I had a morning appointment. He assured me he had no pressing matters that afternoon, so one would be fine. He told me of his favorite bistro uptown near the museum district.

The unexpected aspect of my eating adventure started with my late-morning meeting. It was with an advertising agency president on Madison Avenue. I arrived on time, but the president was running late. By about 11:15 his assistant made regular visits to my waiting room to apologize and to offer coffee and the use of an empty office. I was in no rush, so I worked on my notebook computer and watched the clock.

By about 11:45 the assistant apologized even more profusely, noting that the president was on a multi-continent conference call.

However, he had written a note to her asking that she express his personal regrets to me and insisting that I join him for lunch at his favorite restaurant, just to make amends.

Out he came, minutes before noon, pumped my hand and told me how he looked forward to my review of the meal I was about to have. After a block or two walk, we were seated, and my host was insisting I try the crisp Chardonnay and the salad with exotic ingredients. He got pretty excited about the special fish entrée and the way the chef prepared it.

We talked, and I caught the odd glimpse of the clock. With my mind on Taylor, I called him on my cell phone from the washroom, about quarter to one. He was already in the bistro uptown, but assured me there was no rush. I said I was just finishing my meeting and expecting to arrive just a few minutes late.

In fact, I had to finish a hearty dessert and decaf cappuccino before I could leave. I squeezed my stuffed frame into a cab just after one and called the Ambassador again, indicating I was about to arrive, with traffic being the only unknown. He assured me that all was well and that he would see me when I arrived.

About 20 minutes late, I finally entered the bistro to find Taylor—distinctive curly grey hair, black-rimmed glasses—at the bar sipping a Merlot. I apologized for being late, blaming New York traffic, but was quickly put at ease by one of Canada's most distinguished diplomats.

We sat and chatted, but Taylor quickly turned his enthusiasm to a discussion of the chef and the menu at this bistro. He insisted I try the soup, and highly recommended a meat dish in a great French sauce. Since I'd just eaten, I was willing to accept any recommendation, because none particularly appealed.

The red herring in this story is that at a New York power lunch, you must have social currency—bona fides, stories, something to hold up your end. I'd done a lot of work with diplomats over the years, but Ambassador Taylor knew them all a lot better, so my bona fides only served to justify my presence, but could not exactly entertain someone with his credentials.

But I did have one small story that intrigued my host. I told him how my business partner, Hal Jones, had been dining in Taylor's official residence in Tehran at the exact time that the Americans were hiding in his basement. Hal was the Canadian Broadcasting Corporation's senior correspondent for many years and was stationed in London at the time. Little did he know he was literally sitting right on top of one of the world's great news stories, and hadn't a clue—a journalist's nightmare.

However, just hours after the story of the freeing of the American hostages broke, Hal got a tip that Ambassador Taylor might be in Paris. He rushed over from London and knocked on doors. Among the doors that provided no information was the Canadian Embassy's. But they were so unconvincing, Hal decided to stake the place out—from the comfort of a nearby bistro. Hal was the only journalist on this story who knew what Taylor looked like, so he sprang into action when he spotted the curly grey hair and dark-rimmed glasses walking down the street.

Hal did his interview, including a clip for the French network, and rushed to CBC's Paris office. He fired off his story for the major newscasts, but was almost thrown out of the building by a bureaucrat who accused him of trespassing. This makes sense at the CBC, but that's another story.

So Hal redeemed himself by getting the hottest story of the year, right after missing the hottest story of the year. Recounting this bought me about 10 minutes of credibility with my gracious host, but we continued to eat. Taylor recommended the Merlot with both courses. He then pointed out the crème caramel was a specialty and that I had to try it.

I complied and thoroughly enjoyed my long conversation with a historic Canadian hero that lasted until mid-afternoon. I cabbed it back to my Times Square hotel for a nap before my evening event. That night, as usual on my trips to New York, I took in a play—but this time, no dinner.

PREMIERS SHOULD NEVER DRIVE

Just one more reason to be a passenger...

*When the head of government in British Columbia
got caught drinking and driving on vacation in
Hawaii, an experience I had campaigning with a
candidate who ended up in cabinet came to mind.
This appeared in* The Hill Times *in Ottawa.*

Late one night in a political campaign, I was in the passenger seat
of a car driven by a politician who would soon be in the Cabinet.
We happened upon former Prime Minister John Turner who was out
for a walk. My candidate friend flashed the lights, tooted the horn
and pulled over to say "hello". I rolled down my window so the two
old friends could exchange greetings. Mr. Turner's eyes lit up. The
former PM thrust his finger, arm and head through my window,
across the front of the car and into the face of my politician friend
who was driving.

He admonished, "You shouldn't be driving. If I were running against
you I'd smash into your car and claim you were drunk and hit me".

Good advice. It's a shame B.C. Premier Gordon Campbell wasn't
there to hear it.

Politicians and public figures have long known the rules. John
Turner himself was asked questions about his drinking. He replied
that he "likes a party" but his work was not affected.

But the rules change. For U.S. presidential candidate Gary Hart, an
extra-marital affair ended his campaign. But president Bill Clinton's
confidence ratings went up after revelations about his affairs.

There is speculation that we all hold public figures up to a higher level of scrutiny than ordinary people, in part to compensate for the fact that we live in an amoral society. For those who think "amoral" is exaggeration, take a look at homelessness, abuse of children and hunger. Some years the sale of illegal drugs exceeds the profits of some auto makers. Then there are the recent headlines about executive excess and stock market hyping.

And now, Gordon Campbell has had too much to drink. He has had too much to drink because there is a history of alcoholism in his family, which contributed to his father's suicide. He has had too much to drink because he is a public figure subject to more scrutiny than you or I. Worst of all, he has had too much to drink because he then got into a car and drove.

Those are the public and private rules that Gordon Campbell broke. And he knew the rules.

Other rules were broken in Hawaii too. Mr. Campbell had his three martinis and glasses of wine in the home of his friend Fred Latremouille. Fred is a smart and successful media personality in Vancouver, an intense media town. More than 30 years ago, Fred was causing a stir as a disc jockey. He's had success in commercials, TV hosting and interviewing. A highlight of my short broadcasting career was replacing Fred one summer on CBC-TV's supper hour news. He's seen people skewered in the media, skewered a few himself, and knows better than to serve a friend and public figure three martinis and wine before letting him drive home. Had Mr. Campbell hit someone with his car, both he and Fred could have been liable. There's lots of blame to go around.

But what is to be done? I agree with the work of MADD (Mothers Against Drunk Driving), who have helped radically change attitudes toward this dangerous activity and turn those who do drink and drive into social pariahs.

But should Mr. Campbell be hounded from office? Will that serve a higher social purpose? I think not. If we banish all who drink to excess from positions of responsibility, there will be few journalists, politicians, musicians and business people left standing. Even if we only hound those who drink and drive, we'll lose too many. MADD needs to keep up the pressure to make drinking and driving a completely intolerable activity, and grounds for losing one's license. But B.C. voters didn't elect Gordon Campbell on a temperance ticket. B.C. is entitled to the premier it elected to deal with a range of policy issues that don't involve alcohol.

Certainly Mr. Campbell's actions speak to a lack of judgment. But, again, there would be few leaders left in positions of authority if everyone who showed occasional bad judgment, were ousted.

The rule in crisis management is that the punishment must have a weight and temperature that exceeds the offence.

"I'm sorry" doesn't make up for drunk driving.

Mr. Campbell may be suffering from a serious disease—alcoholism—which some members of his family do. There is no more reason to hound him from office than if he had a cleft lip, club foot or diabetes. He should have begun his news conference by taking the driver's license out of his wallet and cutting it up with scissors. He should have cited his family history and pledged two things: to get professional help and to never drive again while Premier. He should also help MADD do their valuable work. He might just end up being an extremely effective force against the very thing that could bring about his downfall. But he has to act quickly to seize and maintain the initiative.

John Turner was right. Driving even when sober is dangerous for a politician, and Gordon Campbell now has one more reason to be just a passenger.

Pulling the Rug Over Their Eyes

Whether you're called Executive Assistant, Chief of Staff or gopher, part of a political aide's job is public and media relations. I thought I was really on to something when I got a bright idea for a charity auction. In a way it backfired, but in another way, it achieved a purpose my political boss was always interested in—half a page in the newspaper.

This version of the story appeared almost 20 years after the fact in The National Post.

I once made the mistake of suggesting to Mel Lastman that he had been lucky in business. After all, if you're selling fridges and stoves right after Hurricane Hazel and just before a massive immigration influx into Toronto, you're bound to succeed.

Without cracking a smile, Mel flatly said, "the harder you work, the luckier you get".

He worked hard in politics, too. When I was his executive assistant in the early '80s, there was never any mystery in my mind about his success as mayor of North York. He simply arrived every day determined to get in the paper, seize an initiative or make something happen. Everyday.

Some days were better than others. And even when I thought I had a great idea, life with Mel could be unpredictable. One of my great ideas resulted in a huge PR blunder. Late one night, working with Mel in his office, I found one of his old toupées in a drawer while looking for something else.

I remembered that a charity had approached me for something to auction off and I didn't want to give them an old tie.

"Can I give them your old hairpiece?" I asked the Mayor.

"Why not? What do I care?" he answered.

The charity was happy. And I'd shown my boss I could come up with a good idea.

The day after the auction, there was the rug—in several papers! But guess who had bought it? It was Mel's arch-rival, Howard Moscoe, grimacing, holding Mel's former hair at arms' length, and spraying it with Raid or something.

Working for Mel, every day featured a never-ending drumbeat of unusual events:

Item The Pope is visiting North York in 1985, and Mel's preposterous angle is to claim to have figured out that the ratio of faithful to port-a-potties means each person can spend only 35 seconds relieving themselves. Mel tells any reporter who'll listen this amazing statistic.

Item It's 1984, and we've invented a new type of snow plow in North York that docsn't block people's driveways. This gets coverage every year we invent it.

Item Mel plays the bolo-bat and yoyo for 600 grade-school students each year—in his office!

Item We've figured out a way to build the domed stadium in North York—without costing the taxpayers a cent!

And through it all, there was an old Walter Winchell news teletype going inside my head, tapping out the headlines by the minute.

Mel had a committee to fight drunk driving before I'd ever heard of MADD. He knew how many new jobs there would be if we legalized Sunday shopping. He fought the dangers of hitch-hiking and wanted safer cigarettes to prevent house fires and save lives.

I got a steady stream of calls and visits from millionaires, developers, promoters and nuts. An artist wanted to install the world's largest sculpture on the lawn of City Hall. A lawyer knew how to pick up garbage cheaper. A ratepayer fought the dangers of a new building tooth and nail, and then applied to be its security guard when it was approved.

All this came through me. Worthy items were fed to the press daily.

Then there was "The Speech". Mel recited his Bad Boy promotions from long before he was mayor. He'd talk to marketing classes, business luncheons and wherever two or more were gathered in the name of publicity.

In the early days, as Bad Boy, Mel followed ice trucks to see who needed to buy a fridge. He'd give away free bricks of ice cream in hopes people would buy freezers so they wouldn't get covered with the stuff when it melted.

If a shopper wanted to get a coffee and think over a Bad Boy deal, he'd say, "Great, I'll buy, and get me one, too!"

"Then, I'd get another shot at them, when they came back," Mel once boasted to me.

He once claimed to have "sold a refrigerator to an Eskimo... and got paid off in dead fish!" He walked down Yonge Street in a mini-skirt. He dressed up as a bum and begged for quarters. If anybody gave him one, he gave them a $100 bill in return. He got arrested for vagrancy, but bragged about "thousands of dollars in free publicity".

Mel sold $2 bills on the street for $1, got mobbed and caused traffic jams. He did the same in Italy with lira. The punch line for the Italian campaign was, "It's true! Those Italians don't care who they pinch—or where!"

Mel got pulled down the street in a cage, dressed in his Bad Boy prison outfit. He'd pay all comers $5 if they could spend five minutes in there with him.

He once told me to write a press release saying we were putting paddle boats on the lake created by G. Ross Lord Dam (named after a man Mel says he knew well but sometimes called Lord Ross) up at Finch Avenue West and Dufferin Street. Mel wanted me to say we were the only city "in the world" to have boats on a lake "right in the middle of town!" I made the mistake of citing Geneva, New York, Montreal, Vancouver and Regina as cities with lakes in them, but by the second city Mel was on to another topic and we became the only city in the world "of its size" with a lake. (No city had our exact population, and the paddle-boat issue generated more newspaper copy).

Mel moved at 90 miles an hour, but would occasionally let me know I'd done OK. He wouldn't say much, just nod, smile or say "Did you see your article in the paper?"

But he never did mention my bright idea of donating that toupée to the charity auction. He just saw the picture of Howard Moscoe in the paper, put the clipping in the scrap book, and went on to think about how to get in tomorrow's newspaper.

As for Moscoe, he brags about owning the rug to this day.

STRONACH SHOULD HAVE DEBATED HER OPPONENTS

Star candidate and heiress Belinda Stronach has made headlines as a friend of Bill Clinton's, a Conservative leadership candidate, Liberal Cabinet Minister and potential Liberal leadership candidate. This column was written during the first stage of her career, before she crossed the floor to join the Liberals. It appeared in The Hill Times.

Belinda Stronach should have debated her fellow Conservative candidates and could have won. Using peer-reviewed, academic data on how speakers have impact on audiences, I recently analyzed a randomly-selected speech by each candidate. Ms. Stronach ends up winning on several counts.

It's a dictum of communication that a negative is greater than a positive. Negatives should be avoided. Politicians remember Richard Nixon's "I am not a crook," and George Bush's "No new taxes". And the electorate tends to vote for hope and positive messages, rather than negativity.

With this in mind, my researchers and I counted negatives in each candidate's speech and stumbled on just about the most remarkable ratios since we've been doing this work. Belinda Stronach uses about twice as many positive words as negatives. That's very high. Tony Clement uses more than triple. That's even better.

But Stephen Harper is the exact opposite. Mr. Harper's negatives outweigh positives almost two to one. This means that Stephen

Harper could be seen as the angry young man of the campaign, with Belinda Stronach being optimistic and positive. That could be a huge advantage for her.

Then we looked at sentence length. Studies show that even university graduates have trouble with sentences longer than 18 words. In oral communication, shorter is even better. In this study, we saw about the shortest sentences we've ever seen. Stronach's speech averages 13 words per sentence, Clement's 15. Both these candidates have pretty good writers on board. Harper's sentences are acceptable, but a little long at a 21 word average.

All the speeches studied are well under the 15 minute optimum time limit for impact. Tony Clement and Stephen Harper are known as serious, policy-oriented candidates. But Mr. Clement makes the mistake of using too many numbers and Mr. Harper is not conversational. Ms. Stronach could shine in comparison.

Although Ms. Stronach has been criticized for not having command of policy, that's often not important in a leader's debate. A landmark U.S. study by almost two dozen academics called the Presidential Debates (Praeger, 1980) shows that the issues that come up in a debate are rarely the ones that are important months later after the election. Voters are wise to choose a candidate who looks as if s/he can handle unspecified issues that are not even on the horizon. So, in this context, while the men slug it out on the issue of the day, Ms. Stronach might have scored points for vision. To be sure, she needs a good briefing on issues, but there's no shortage of expert lawyers and professors to volunteer for that role in campaigns.

Studies also show that non-verbal communication can amount for 50 to 75 per cent of impact. Ms. Stronach scores well on facial expressions and body language. She smiles, albeit sometimes a nervous smirk, and leans into her audience showing involvement. She needs work on eye contact and must stop gripping the podium and lift her hands to gesture.

Mr. Clement is better on gestures. They are active without being nervous. They are large and slow for television. *The Journal of Psychology* of November 1998 reports that if a speaker gestures, s/he speaks more clearly, with the message being understood and retained longer by an audience. Mr. Clement does well in these areas, but needs more definitive eye contact. If you can't look at the reporter, audience, or camera (double-enders, videographers) in the eye, you will not be believable.

Mr. Harper has a subdued delivery and needs more lively gestures and body language. We sampled one speech per candidate and video clips at random. No campaign was enthusiastic about providing video tape, and at this writing, none has arrived and one camp has not returned calls.

To be sure, delegate and voter behavior is also highly influenced by issues, name recognition, region and voting history. But for Belinda Stronach, she should go to her strengths and debate the other leaders.

GETTING OUT THE VOTE

There are too many mercenaries for hire in politics. There's too much money. There are too many people hoping to reach into the pork-barrel after the election. There's too much technology and there's too much TV.

Yet, on election day, in many jurisdictions, especially in the Parliamentary system, political power is vested in ordinary people for a few hours. Many of these are the people who put up signs, staffed phone banks and stood at plant gates or bus stops with the candidate during the campaign. Now they staff their own kitchen table, basement or rented campaign office in what was a failed pizza parlor that nobody else wanted to rent.

On election day, it boils down to getting out the vote. Calls, offers of a lift to the voting place and watching over the democratic process as electors vote are a high calling. This is the best homage to that calling I can muster.

The process begins the minute the election is called. Campaigners go door to door to start to identify the vote. Others are doing the same by phone. In a winter campaign there may be more reliance on the phone because of weather.

The main purpose of the door to door canvass and the candidate canvass is not discussing policy or even introducing the candidate to the electorate. Candidates have been all but irrelevant in North

American elections for over 100 years. The purpose of the candidate canvass is to tell the people who are not home that the candidate was there. That voter will assume the candidate met almost all the others in the neighborhood. The purpose of the other canvass, minus the candidate, is just to identify the vote, not drop off simplistic literature. The conversation at the door can be dressed up with all kinds of folderol about issues, lawn signs, skateboards on sidewalks, the national campaign and so on, but the only exchange that matters is:

"Have you decided how you're gong to vote?"

Some voters tell you. Others signal that the secret ballot is important to them. Others pretend to be undecided or perhaps really are. The trick is to guess who is who and mark it down on a form.

Election day volunteers in the campaign office call the voters who are in their party and make sure the vote gets out. Volunteers offer a drive, if necessary. But, for the most part, committed voters will vote regardless. There's often a lot of boredom on election day. There may be a few older people and shift workers at home, but the real action starts about 5 p.m. and doesn't end until the polls close.

One big problem is that for the several weeks before voting day, it's a volunteer army that's creating these lists. In some campaigns, volunteers are lucky to have any list and to be able to read the notations on the ones that exist.

There can be 300 polls in a riding or district. Each party can supply an inside and outside scrutineer in each poll. The inside scrutineer sits in the polling place, marks off and sometimes challenges voters. A challenge occurs if the party worker thinks the voter has voted twice or is not registered. Outside workers can go in and check the list to see who has voted. The Deputy Returning Officer & Poll Clerk are paid by the government and they often don't like people looking over their shoulders to find out who has voted.

However, party workers need to determine who has voted, in order to tell their volunteer cohorts back in the campaign office, so the ones who haven't can be called and cajoled into voting.

A typical riding needs two volunteers per poll and a phone bank of as many people as one can get. Rarely, if ever, does a campaign have all the people it needs. A good team can get out several hundred votes or even up to a thousand.

Only close ridings are affected by this so called "ground game", but a few close ridings can sometimes turn an election or beef up a regional caucus.

ANAMATICS

Competitive advantage can be achieved in a political campaign through better use of a blackboard and chalk, more phone lines for the phone bank, more volunteer drivers and/or better use of new technology. We're never sure which technological wave will stick and which one will affect the outcome of a particular campaign. I speculated about such things after reviewing candidate and party web pages for the network television program "Politics", hosted by Don Newman.

A recent all candidates' debate during a national leaders' campaign got me thinking about one of my pet peeves—research. Below, I offer some upgrades to the unscientific focus group—a mainstay of modern research.

I was just asked to review the performances of 11 politicians in an all candidates' debate months before voting. Since anything can happen in even a month in politics, I struggled with what perspective I would offer on a TV show called "Politics".

Issues could change, candidates can drop out, scandals can hit and so on. I saw little point in reviewing content and policy so early in a campaign. I remembered an old technique from focus groups. It sometimes pays to show a candidate talking on video with no sound and get reactions to the body language only. The specific information respondents produce, based on watching a silent picture of a candidate speaking, is revealing. They are reacting to eye contact, facial expressions, speaking versus listening time and intensity in listening, among many other factors.

I asked the TV network to pull short clips of all candidates, so I could review them in split screen with no sound. Each was speaking with the audience or debating other candidates.

Here's what we found. First, several candidates were spending most of their time reading. If you have to read "Good evening ladies and gentlemen, I'm pleased to be here with you"—you have a real problem. Surely you can remember you're pleased to be somewhere. Live audiences and TV viewers will not vote for the top of a candidate's head while the head reads a speech.

The next thing that was obvious, was that some candidates did not appear to be comfortable in their own skin. This seems to be an intangible matter, but audiences know it when they see it. A stiff delivery, awkward gestures, fidgeting, pacing and other things that would put you off at a party, also put audiences off in large political venues. Conversely, a candidate who can step to the side of the podium, reach out with a natural double hand gesture, look at ease and smile, has a huge advantage over those who cling to the podium and script.

The value of testing politicians' performances with no sound is just one way to get more value out of a focus group. Another is anamatics. That's a catch-all word that means make the testing as close to reality as possible.

Here's how it can work in politics. Most focus groups sit eight to ten people around a board room table while a client watches from behind two-way mirrors. Depending on what you're testing, this can be such an unrealistic atmosphere that you don't really learn much.

Take campaign literature, householders or direct mail pieces. People don't sit around a board room table with strangers, reacting to paper being passed around the table. How about throwing the odd mail piece or brochure on the floor with a bunch of other mail and see if anyone picks it up? How about leaving a bunch of material on the board room table and leaving the participants alone to see if any of them show any interest in the stuff? If not, you have a big problem that asking their opinions of the graphics won't fix.

My New York partner, Ken Kansas, helped invent anamatics during decades of high end attitudinal research, directing ad agencies and funding civic arts projects. He advocates testing a TV commercial in graphic story-board treatment only. Audiences are sophisticated enough to review production techniques and ignore the content. What are you electing, a video editor, graphic artist or a candidate? Story boards cause an audience to review the steak, not just the sizzle.

Then, instead of showing test audiences the commercial in a false setting like a board room, how about a room set up like a living room with a couch, newspapers and other distractions normally found in the home? This might test whether people are interested in the commercial at all.

How about actually using someone's basement TV room into which the homeowner invites all the neighbors? How about stripping the ad into the actual TV show in which it will run and surrounding it with other ads so the audience's reaction is tested in a realistic setting? Ken used to take such ads to shopping centres and run hundreds of people through a room over a few days to get a large sample and increase the reliability of the data.

Since Ken did his work, new technology presents new possibilities. Focus group respondents can be picked up in a van equipped with video screens. As they are being driven to the alleged focus group room, they can be shown a real TV show with the ads to be tested stripped in. During the drive, the people can be watched to see how much attention they pay. Once in the focus group room, they can be debriefed on what they remember. If it's nothing, it's back to the drawing board. There's no point in making them look at an ad and react to it if they wouldn't voluntarily watch it. The same technique can be used with even better results with radio ads in the van, since it's more realistic to listen to the radio than watch TV in a vehicle.

In industry, empathic testing means using a real person in a real kitchen to test a real coffee pot. There are documented cases of manufacturers learning valuable lessons that save or make them millions.

The lesson in politics is surely that the candidate should be tested in realistic circumstances too. Whatever else motivates voters, they are surely voting to put that candidate in their living room TV sets multiple times per week over the duration of the mandate. So, it's in real living rooms, in real TV programs that the candidate should be tested.

NEGATIVITY

George Shipley is a great character to work with, fly with, dine with, and chat with. I'm glad to say I've had all those pleasures, many times.

Texas political consultant George Shipley is mad as hell, but he's going to keep taking it and dishing it out. He's mad at the mindless, anti-democratic death sport that American politics has become.

I've done work with Dr. Shipley, and he's smart. He's also ruthless when he has to be. He's also a rare breed—a Texas Democrat.

George starts with the money. A credible campaign for Governor will cost $30 million. A Senator will spend that getting re-elected. Most of that money will be spent on TV.

George calls TV the "counter campaign". While you try to build up your candidate's brand, you are expending a huge effort to destabilize your opponent's brand. You better go into a campaign with a great brand, because negative works and positive doesn't.

What works in the negative is every trick in the book. Ridicule, irony, innuendo and outright lies work very well. This media campaign can be backed up with phone banks and direct mail. George has seen campaigns where ads have referenced the Easter Bunny and Tinker Bell to imply the candidate is gay. He's seen a Latino candidate being associated with violence and even virtually accused of murder because it plays into horrible and inaccurate racial stereotypes.

It used to be that you had to be careful of negative ads. They could backfire. This is still true where campaign spending limits prevent massive TV buys, but where money is no object and the campaign is long, you just keep buying TV time.

Conventional wisdom used to be that you had to use your negatives early in a campaign to get voters' attention. Then, you followed up quickly with a positive vision of what you would do to solve the problems you told everybody existed.

The real problem with negativity is that it has worked. It has defeated and elected many candidates, depending on who's using the ad. But the other way negativity has worked has perhaps been unintended. Studies show that negatives breed a negative environment. While critical campaigns may work in the short term, after a couple of campaigns, voters forget who they hate the most and end up hating all politicians.

Big deal, some would say; negativity got the job done. But in the long term, the entire brand *politician* has gone in the dumpster. Many years and campaigns, during which talented operatives like George Shipley have been crying wolf have caused the electorate to polarize and distrust all politicians. The consequences are huge.

To consider how huge, cast your mind back to the movie "Mr. Smith Goes to Washington". An idealistic young politician goes to the nation's capital and really makes a difference, with support from a letter-writing campaign from constituents, including the Boy Scouts. Cast your non-partisan mind back to President Eisenhower's military industrial complex speech, which was his heartfelt warning and gift to the American people. In it he prophetically warned of inflation when it was at low single digits, and of the military and industrial machine gaining too much influence. A few years later, President Kennedy made speeches thanking the American people for their sacrifices. Paying higher taxes and working harder were going to help send a man to the moon, win the cold war and break up monopolistic critical industries.

Now, it's hard to imagine any politician demanding a sacrifice of the electorate. What sacrifices has the average American been asked to make since 9/11? Food, gas, rubber or other rationing? Speed limits or indoor temperature limits as President Nixon mandated after the first energy crunch? Nixon even had a policy initiative to require Detroit to make a car that got good gas mileage, was affordable and was either recyclable or didn't use scarce material. We could use that initiative now. How about nuclear? We could have plants coming on stream by now if they'd been started the week after 9/11.

The other thing that's hard to imagine is anyone believing a politician if s/he asked us to make a sacrifice, or told us what was important in the world. We'd be rightly skeptical because of all politicians' past performances.

THE DIGITAL DIVIDE

Twenty-five years ago I moved into an historic political jurisdiction. Ontario Conservatives held power for 42 years, which is a record in western democracies. I'd spend most of my life living thousands of miles away, so had few pre-conceptions about the parties and candidates.

After settling in, I watched news reports of government and candidate activity and the reason for the electoral longevity was a bit of a mystery. But then an election was called. The first thing I noticed was that one party was way ahead in TV ad production. They weren't outstanding, but they did stand out in a mediocre field.

Opposition candidates were using tacky TV studio mock ups. One ad featured a candidate (Liberal Stuart Smith) standing beside a helium cylinder, blowing up balloons. The message may have been something about puffed up promises. Another candidate (New Democrat Michael Cassidy) jammed himself into a fake grocery store set to complain about the high cost of canned peaches. But the set was so small that when it came time to wheel his shopping cart out, he had to just jiggle it back and forth and pretend to leave. The net result of both ads was to transmit a sense of unreal chicanery.

Meanwhile the governing party of 42 years had upbeat music, shots of smiling, happy people and candidates as well as a generic, positive message.

At the time, I made some quick predictions that I'm willing to stand by, twenty five years later. First, I said that the party or

---

candidate that caught up and matched the governing party in its TV production skills would level the playing field and turn the elections into a fair fight. (Within five years there had been a change of government).

Second, I said that the party or candidate that first mastered high definition TV would have a serious competitive advantage over all others. As of this writing, the High Definition TV (HDTV) penetration in the home is just enough to make my prediction true, and there's new technology that is allowing me to recycle my opinion.

I have just been to the IdeaCity06 conference—a gathering of people with big brains and big hearts in Toronto. One of the presenters talked about how Hollywood is being transformed by the digital revolution. Here's the background. Even if Hollywood movies are shot on film, they are instantly transferred to digital. Why? Film is more expensive to transport and copy, it's more fragile, can't be sent around on the web, and can't be manipulated as easily as digital.

Manipulated is one of those words that attracts the attention of politicos—and for good reason. The cost saving and portability is attractive to political campaigns. But so should be the quality of digital, which is now a combination of HDTV and 3D. If 3D gets you thinking of old 1950s horror movies, think again. I just saw a demonstration of the latest version and it's fantastic. It looks like the best moving View-Master or stereo picture you've ever seen, and soon may be available without those colored glasses needed in the first round of 3D movies.

What are the political implications, other than you have to get into this game? First, follow the money. Every Hollywood studio has several new digital movies in the works. They will soon be outfitting theatres with the technology to play these remarkable images. Why? It's for the same reason Hollywood got into stereo, wide screen, smell-o-vision and 3D in the 1950s—to compete. In the 1950s the competition was TV. Now it's computers, hand-helds and video games.

Because of competition, most theatres have very slow nights on Mondays and Tuesdays. The new theatres that are retrofitted for digital will be rented out for special events. One of them could be a high-tech version of the old *self-liquidating vehicle*.

One of the best uses of this technique was made by Ronald Reagan's campaigns. A known and screened Republican would be sent a video tape, brochures and other campaign materials. S/he would be appointed *block captain* or some other important-sounding title. This person would invite people from the neighborhood to view the video and get the campaign literature at a social evening in the person's home. The reason this vehicle was called self-liquidating is that the attendees would be asked to pay for the privilege of attending the campaign evening.

Fast forward to the 500 3D enabled theatres that will be converted in eighteen months, and you can see the possibilities; hundreds instead of dozens can attend. The digital campaign movie can be sent out on the web for pennies. It can also feature this remarkable new 3D, high-definition quality. On the off chance some audience members aren't attracted by the candidate or party, it will still be mandatory to experience this new leap forward in visual images.

In this new venue, the candidate will appear real. S/he can reach out literally and figuratively to the audience. There will be a metaphorical and actual depth, color and shape to the candidate and campaign which TV reports. I'm not entirely sure what advantage this will bring, but I'd rather have the new technology than fight it.

Other applications will include special flat screen stereo TVs in public areas and soon in homes. Existing flat screen TVs can soon be equipped with converter boxes and glasses so viewers can see the new 3D images. Political campaigns will also be well advised to get into short promos and commercials for use in movie theatres and on TV.

Meanwhile, there's no free lunch. This will create challenges. A special 3D camera is required. There are new rules for composition, taking into account a distinct foreground, middle ground and background to show off the 3D effect. Talking pictures made some actors and politicians sound ridiculous with high squeaky voices. High Definition will require performance adjustments. As in the Kennedy-Nixon debate in 1960, makeup techniques will change. So will proper clothing and gestures when the digital image shows more depth and side views. How much of a change in candidate behavior will be required is a guess, but if I were a 2008 Presidential hopeful, I'd be testing how I looked and acted in digital.

THE DIGITAL DIVIDE

Focus Groups

I've written often about the concerns I have with research techniques. This column was inspired by my attendance at a focus group.

I was just asked to attend some focus groups and I was reminded of the dozen or so reasons I don't like them.

First, rich and busy people usually won't attend, skewing data to a narrow demographic. This would taint research in a decent under-graduate social science class. Worse, focus group companies know where they can get repeat attendees on short notice. These are often students, the unemployed or at least people who live near the focus group facilities. All of this taints the data too.

In this particular focus group I feel a twinge as soon as the leader walks in the room. She is too talkative, as if trying to entertain a client, not conduct research. Conducting professional scientific research is a learned skill. Notice I use the term *scientific* and do not make a distinction with social science.

About fifty years ago Heisenberg said that the instrument used in a laboratory experiment affects the results of the experiment—the *Heisenberg uncertainty principle*. A thermometer used to measure temperature changes the temperature of the thing it's measuring. In 1962, Kuhn pointed out that scientists have a tendency to collect data that supports their views and ignore that which conflicts. He used the term *paradigms* to describe this phenomenon. Merton and Feyerabend discussed how science is a value-laden pursuit, driven by those performing the science.

So the focus group leader is in a difficult position; waltzing in like the star of the show, trying to impress, performing for the client behind the two-way mirror or any other false behavior, can make that position untenable and skew the data.

A focus group leader should dress and talk one step up from the subjects in the room. S/he is there for scientific purposes to gather data, not make friends or entertain.

Most focus groups begin much too quickly. The leader should allow discussion to evolve slowly with open ended questions to see what the respondents want to discuss. Closed, specific questions, especially ones that can be answered with "yes", or "no", or a short sentence, won't reveal as much as an open ended question encouraging discussion.

Closed questions yield what researchers call an *aided* response. The questions tell respondents what to talk about. Open questions yield an *unaided* response, where the respondents can tell researchers what to think about—the way it should be!

In the focus group I was in recently, we were testing confidential matters. But let's say it was reactions to Candidate X. One of the first questions was, "What kind of car do you think Candidate X drives?"

This sparks a discussion of myriad types of cars. I'm reminded that some people follow car models more than others. Some may name one car thinking it's the sportiest on the market, while another person may name the same model because it represents fuel efficiency, economy or some other attribute.

In the end, without knowing what respondents mean by the car models they name, you end up with a mish-mash of information that could mean anything. "Cadillac" means luxury, high-price, high fuel consumption and perhaps the ability of American industry to compete with anyone on the planet. Who knows?

But if there really were to be value in the car question, it should have begun in an open ended fashion such as, "How does Candidate X get around the district or campaign trail?"

Respondents might name trains, boats, planes and cars. If we find out people think the candidate flies around in a private jet, that could be a problem. If cars are really relevant, after an open discussion of other types of travel, the closed ended question could be asked about what kind of car the candidate uses.

In the focus group I watched, one respondent got up on his hind legs and said he didn't think the candidate used a car. It takes guts to challenge an authority figure and say the question is wrong. If a respondent does that, it's a very powerful message that you could be on the wrong track.

Next the leader holds up pages from the candidate's web page, passes them around and asks for a review. That's not how people use web pages, so it's hard to tell what was being tested.

Next, the leader passes around literature that the candidate regularly sends out. The question was, "What do you like about the brochures, householders and other communication?"

I have two problems with this line of questioning. First, it misses the opportunity to find out if anybody remembers getting anything in the mail from the candidate. People may feel boxed into saying they received and remembered the material, when the most valuable information might be that they didn't. Next, what if people hate the literature? Asking what they like about it, cuts off the discussion about what they don't like.

People like to be cooperative when being paid, so you have to be careful they aren't so cooperative that you don't find out what they're really thinking.

Next came the Barbara Walters question. She was famous for asking an interviewee, "If you were a tree, what kind of tree would you be?"

In this session, respondents were shown pictures of all kinds of people—young, old, various races, both genders and so on. As they are looking at the pictures, the leader asks, "If the candidate's campaign were a person, what person would it be?"

Not only is the question a bit odd, it's hard to tell what people mean when they pick a picture of a fit, muscular looking man. Does mean the campaign is intimidating, full of thugs, or has staying power for the long run? Next, respondents start answering questions that weren't asked. One picks the construction worker because the candidate comes from a part of the district where there's lots of construction. Another picks the young Asian woman because the district is becoming more multi-cultural. Some seem to be picking people they find attractive or would like to be with, not who embody the campaign. This ends in another mish-mash of unusable information.

I innocently asked the client where the pictures came from? It turns out employees of the research company picked them. They may use them every session, for all I know. Regardless, it does not make a lot of sense to me to have respondents judging pictures picked either at random or purposefully by a research company to make their sessions go more smoothly.

Next, the leader asks what does each person in the picture do for a living, and what does each person do on weekends? (I assume the construction worker works in construction).

Ironically, after going to all this trouble to stimulate fairly irrelevant discussion, the leader cuts off dialogue by asking if anyone has any final thoughts? When the leader leaves the room to get more instructions from the client, I listen in to the continuing discussion in the focus group room. It's actually a better discussion, unaided by the leader. One older woman began waxing nostalgic about the district, the party and the candidate.

So, what's the right approach? There are lots of them. Credible scientists use several different methods and compare them to obtain more reliable data. Polls, questionnaires, elite interviews with opinion leaders and lay-elite dialogues to see where there are gaps between those in the know and regular folks, can all help. So can old-fashioned research. Online databases now make it really easy to search everything from newspapers to academic journals. For all a campaign knows, five distinguished academics and journalists have written 10,000 excellent words on the topic over the years.

Focus groups can be helpful, if run properly. But they also need to be augmented with sound, old-fashioned research, preferably in libraries, surrounded by books.

MAKING THE BEST OF
MEDIA INTERVIEWS

This is one of my earliest columns, written for Bout de Papier *in the 1980s. Even though I disagree with the combative advice that Hannaford gives in his book, I'm pleased with how well the overall piece stands up.*

Note the dated reference to tainted tuna which caused a political and business crisis in Canada.

Note also the better known reference to Tylenol. This case is still discussed in universities and conferences, including at Harvard courses I've attended. Someone laced the painkiller with poison and seven people died. Many professors teach that the Exxon Valdez oil spill was one of the worst environmental disasters in history, and that the Tylenol case was a great example of effective crisis management.

I have a different message in my lectures. Sixty per cent of Exxon Valdez oil evaporated within six hours of the spill. Oil is biodegradable and government scientists had trouble finding any of it just two years later. No one was killed. It was not terrorism. There were record fish catches in the two years following the spill. While many living organisms were killed, no species was affected over time. The worst injury may have been a broken ankle and headaches.

While the Tylenol case was well handled, there are other lessons to learn. Johnson and Johnson were the victims of terrorism, which made public reaction entirely different than if they'd been the cause. The lesson many take from the case is that you should always say you're sorry and pull the product. This ruined Dow Beer in the late sixties, severely harmed Ball Park Hot Dogs in a product tampering case that proved to be a hoax, and could have hurt Pepsi when people wrongly claimed to have found syringes in their cans of soda.

The other thing I've tried to test with people who teach the two cases is the issue of values. If recapturing 98 per cent of a $75 million market is success, then Tylenol had it. If it's prevention, that's another matter. Historically, there is a case of product tampering about every week in North America. This may have gone down since the Tylenol poisonings, but perhaps all food and drug manufacturers should have made their products harder to tamper with long before this event. At least 5,000 people in America die every year from food poisoning, so general cleanliness in preparation and food storage are important issues too.

I note that no one has been caught, tired or convicted of this crime. That's part of crisis management. I also don't hear professors discussing the loved ones of the seven victims, all of whom were relatively young people. I assume there are a hundred grieving friends and relatives, and I have

*not heard their story. I have not heard the story of
what the families may have gone through in their
grieving process or how their loss was addressed.
All this may have been handled well too, but I note
that PR conference speakers, as well as business
and legal professors do not find this an important
topic. As long as the crisis management focus is on
advertising, 800 phone numbers, technical skill in
recalling the product, media interviews and such,
the full lesson of this and other events will not have
been taught.*

*But, in the 1980s my focus was on the technical
skill needed for media interviews, and there is still a
big appetite for these matters in politics and the
diplomatic corps.*

Being a successful media performer now appears to be an integral part of a successful communications strategy. But for the professional communicator there are unfortunately very few places to turn for expert advice on being a good media performer. Most PR books deal with press releases and lists, and many companies specializing in training don't possess the range of skills needed to "arm" a senior executive or administrator. Ex-journalists, for example, are often good at asking questions, but sometimes lack the skills to teach clients how to answer questions. Often, trainers lack a policy or theoretical background.

However, two publications define skills senior people need when dealing with the media, and help in choosing a consultant to hone media skills. These books may prove to be as valuable on your shelf as they might have to executives at Johnson and Johnson (makers of Tylenol) or Starkist Tuna.

A section of *Business-Government Relations in Canada* by Professor W.T. Stanbury (Methuen, Toronto 1986) offers advice for would-be media performers. The book is not so much written, as compiled. There's no real narrative, but dozens of lists and bullet points. The many summaries of social science data and studies make this book the last word on the topic, but with 678 pages and a dry style, you have to be really interested in the words.

Stanbury has listed the basic reasons why business people (or public administrators) don't get along with the media:

- Business people are used to being the boss, but in public life, the media is the boss.
- Reporters may be personally but not professionally intimidated by "officials".
- Reporters are often not a high priority for administrators.
- Reporters need immediate high level access, which many senior people are not used to giving.
- The media does distort by its nature...albeit through a benign distortion of simplification, amplification, and the use of examples.
- Reporters judge a story on its interest, not on whether it's good for the administrator or organization being written about.

He also offers a list of the eight classic interview pitfalls (applying mainly to television, but useful for radio and print as well). He adds a few dirty questions often asked by interviewers, and the appropriate response:

1. The set up (a long preamble that's a loaded question).

   RESPONSE: Challenge the premise, don't nod your head during the question, but do state your positive version of the facts.

2. The "either...or" question where both alternatives are unacceptable.

   RESPONSE: Don't attack the questioner, but say "neither" and state the true situation.

3. The irrelevancy...a question unrelated to your field or topic.

   RESPONSE: Acknowledge the question, but quickly bridge to your communications objective.

4. The Empty Chair (a quote from someone not present).

   RESPONSE: Don't argue with someone who isn't there to defend his or her position. Say you haven't seen or heard the remarks and bridge to your own message.

5. The Broadside ("You're a polluter, aren't you?").

   RESPONSE: Don't get fazed. Say "No" in a nice but forceful way and bridge to your message.

6. The "What If?" question...

    RESPONSE: Don't speculate or try to predict the future, but say, "That raises the real issue of..." and state your case.

7. The inconsistency.

    RESPONSE: If your company has been inconsistent, admit it, but show the consistency within the inconsistency.

8. No comment...don't use it. This remark cuts off the conversation and is just plain rude.

One of the only books completely dedicated to improving the reader's chances of surviving ambush or hostile interviews is *Talking Back to the Media*. (It's New York publisher, Facts on File, has some other interesting titles dealing with the media, i.e. *Would You Put That In Writing & Media Controversies*). Author Peter Hannaford takes a rather confrontational approach to media relations in *Talking Back*, but considering his background (former director of Public Affairs for Ronald Reagan) and some recent revelations about the techniques of journalists, his approach is worth knowing about.

The revelations cited are:

1. Former *Ramparts* editor, Warren Hinckle is quoted as saying, "What journalism is all about is to attack everybody. First you decide what's wrong, then you go out to find the facts to support that view, and then you generate enough controversy to attract attention".

2. Journalist Janet Cooke published a story about an 8-year-old heroin addict in the *Washington Post*. The story was up for a Pulitzer Prize when Ms. Cooke finally confessed to fabricating the story.

3. *New York Daily News* columnist Michael Daly admits to inventing a British soldier who shot a Northern Ireland teenager in cold blood. Daly admitted to altering facts in other columns as well.

4. A *New York Times Sunday Magazine* story by free-lance writer Christopher Jones, purporting to be an eyewitness account of conditions in Cambodia, had actually been concocted in the comfort of his own home in Spain. Parts of the story had been lifted from a 1930 novel by André Malraux.

5. "60 Minutes" accused Los Angeles physician Carl Galloway of involvement in a scheme to defraud health insurance companies. Galloway sued. On the witness stand, CBS' Dan Rather said he'd put in several calls to the doctor which were not returned. Rather stated that in his experience, failure to return a call tended to confirm his suspicion about the subject of the investigation.

6. New York writer Alastair Reid admitted to having used fiction in ostensibly factual articles on a number of occasions dating back to 1961.

Meanwhile Fred Friendly, former president of CBS news and emeritus professor at Columbia's Graduate School of Journalism, and Edward R. Murrow's ex-producer, simply denounces any inaccuracies by saying, "A composite is a euphemism for a lie. It's disorderly, it's dishonest, and it's not journalism".

The book offers a more comprehensive approach than the analysis that journalists are people too and make mistakes. It offers a prescription for avoiding being a victim of those human mistakes. For example, Hannaford adds four new items to the list of what to do and remember when you're being interviewed:

1. Don't repeat the accuser's allegations (i.e. say "I'm honest", not "I am not a crook").

2. Ask questions yourself.

3. Remember you're not having a casual conversation with an old friend—be cautious and avoid flippancy.

4. Have a SOCO—That's a single overriding communications objective that you return to, regardless of the question asked (my company is doing even more in the future to avoid pollution).

An extremely useful lesson is to remember to offer your premise first and then answer the question. Barry Goldwater didn't know this, so his reflex "nuke 'em" answers were what got reported, not the mild discussion that followed. Ronald Reagan learned the lesson though. Reagan used to say "No" to the question "Do you favor the Equal Rights Amendment?" This sounded anti-feminist, abrupt and negative. Reagan then learned to set up the answer like this:

"I support equal rights for women. The ERA is one approach. I think there is a better one. In recent years there have been important changes in federal and state laws to ensure equal pay for equal work and other rights for women. We need to look at our statutes to find out where discrimination against women still exists and change those that do. The ERA, on the other hand, would result in years of tangled court cases. We can resolve the remaining equal rights questions much more quickly by changing any laws that stand in the way of equality".

In part for the humor content, Hannaford offers the four defences to trick questions:

1. "I didn't do it".

2. "I did it, but there was a good reason".

3. "I did it. I'm sorry. I was wrong and I've learned from my mistake".

4. "Whoever says I did such a thing is a low-down, good-for-nothing bum" (or similar epithet). Follow this with a counter attack on your accuser—if you have the facts to back it up.

Talking Back to the Media offers several excellent case studies as well. One is the Coors case. When the beer company with a bad reputation got a call from Mike Wallace, the VP for Corporate Public Relations didn't get sick or stonewall. He spent $60,000 preparing for the encounter. Media training was a big part of the strategy, and the company scored a landmark PR triumph that helped turn Coors' image around, lessen the effects of a growing boycott by union supporters and apparently increased sales. In fact, the Coors people lobbied "60 Minutes" to rerun the item the summer after it was first broadcast.

The final case study worth a spot in Public Affairs professionals' files concerns crisis management. It involves a copycat scare following the Tylenol case. This one was in Detroit where several people put foreign objects (including half a razor blade) in sealed packages of hot dogs. The company reacted too quickly with partial information, but made a spectacular recovery by being honest and open with the media and its consumers. Sales increased as a result, whereas the company could have suffered huge losses or even bankruptcy.

The lists in both books are equally good. They start the reader thinking about the communication process and what to watch out for. I'd just add a few other points:

1. Look at every contact with the media as an opportunity to get your message out.

2. Study media formats and reporters, and read everything from light memoirs to heavy anthropological studies to find out more about the media.

3. Never forget you're talking to a journalist.

4. Don't be afraid of silence—don't fill the gap with a gaff, just smile and wait for the next question.

5. Don't argue ethics or efficacy with a journalist. Reform the media on your own time—you're just doing your organization harm by attacking the media.

6. Remember the setting you're in—the background may get on TV or be described on radio or in print.

7. Give reporters the best briefing materials your company can produce. It'll show up in the story.

8. Take bad press in stride—it's sure to come eventually.

Both these books underline the importance of television to companies, governments and lobby groups. It's not too simplistic or even superficial to say it's not what you say, but how you say it and how you convey it, that counts in the electronic age. There are dozens or more sociological ways of saying it, and lots of die-hards who wish it weren't so, but those are the facts.

Pugnacious Pierre—Trudeau

This account originally appeared in Law Times.
*I am re-reading it shortly after a new Liberal
leader, Stéphane Dion has taken over his party
after a convention that was probably more exciting than the 1968 event that Mr. Trudeau won on
the fourth ballot.*

*Trivia buffs will remember this was just one of three
celebrated altercations Mr. Trudeau had. While
Prime Minister, he had a famous shoving match
with reporter Jim Munson, now a Senator. After
leaving office, he kicked a TV interviewer in the
groin for clowning around with him too much.*

For almost exactly thirty-seven years, that famous silhouette of
Prime Minister Pierre Trudeau has been staring down at me from
a frame on my wall. The silhouette is a 1960s icon in Canadian
politics. Its main use was as a poster in Trudeau's successful 1968
leadership bid. It was resurrected 16 years later at his farewell
speech—perhaps his or any politicians' best.

The reason this image has been scrutinizing my mundane office
work is that it's on the menu from a famous fundraising dinner at
Seaforth Armoury in Vancouver. It was 1969 and I was a young
teenager taken as a guest by my father, Harold Bonner.

Harold was trying to rebuild the waterfront in a doomed effort
called Project 200 and attended the dinner as part of a general

lobbying effort. The reason the dinner is famous is that it ended in the Prime Minister getting charged with common assault. Remember?

Here's how the event looked from the inside. The Prime Minister came in, made a few remarks, left for a short while, came back, borrowed my fork because he'd missed dinner, ate and left for good.

Here's how it looked from the outside. There was a protest about something or other going on. In fact, it was probably about a number of things—Vietnam, jobs, legalizing marijuana and Trudeau himself. Protesting was a bit of a sport in those days and any excuse would do.

At any rate, Trudeau decided to walk out into the crowd and reason with them. He stepped up on a soap box or something and tried to talk things over with the crowd. It became apparent that the protesters would not quiet down and listen, so the Prime Minister decided to go back inside and borrow my fork.

As Trudeau began parting the crowd and meandering through, he ended up face to face with a 17 year old kid who'd hitchhiked across the country to experience Vancouver in the summer of '69. Not knowing what to say, the kid looked into those steely eyes and said to the Prime Minister, "faggot".

Judo Black Belt Trudeau instantly hauled off and punched the kid right in the nose. He fell back into the arms of several reporters. The evening, both on the inside and outside, proceeded without further incident.

A couple of days later, a reporter found the kid in a drop-in centre and incited him to press charges against Trudeau. By the time the kid tried to retain a good lawyer, the best in town were tied up by the other side. They got Trudeau off on some technicality like extenuating circumstances or the Prime Minister's fear for his safety.

Few thought more of the incident for a while until a couple of days past the kid's 18th birthday. A friend knocked at the door with another guy in tow. They asked to buy some LSD. The kid had a grand total of four tabs for personal use. He told them a couple of times that he did not want to sell any, but the house guests persisted. When the kid gave in, out came the friend of a friend's badge and the arrest went down. The kid was charged with trafficking.

At a time when serious pushers were given two years less a day, he was sentenced to two years plus a day, so he had to do harder time at Oakalla Prison. He was beaten up every other week for about a year until he was offered Outward Bound, the wilderness school, for his last year.

When I tracked the kid down decades later, he was back in small town Ontario, very hopeful about a move to a new community and a new start in construction. I had the impression things had not gone well for him, and felt a twinge of irony, even guilt about how well things had gone for me over the years.

But the kid was middle aged now and had little rancor over the matter. He does not blame the former Prime Minister. He assumes some individual police officers decided to pursue the matter vigorously. He credits Outward Bound with turning his life around.

Considering Pierre Trudeau's early days as an agitator and asbestos protester, I bet he would have sympathized with the kid.

CONTROLLING THE CRISIS CLIMATE

This article is an early one from Bout de Papier. *The crisis management field has evolved since the 1980s, but I'm still pleased with the core advice below.*

One always wishes for greater age, wisdom, insight or argumentative powers in crisis cases, but what is really needed is a formal crisis management plan. Such a plan need not anticipate the actual cause of the crisis, but it should contain policy statements and logistical procedures to reduce the trauma or paralysis of dealing with a crisis. There are two excellent books on the topic which I recommend: *Crisis Management* by Steven Fink, Amacom, 1986 (Prentice-Hall in Canada) and *When You are the Headline* by Robert B. Irvine, Dow Jones Irwin, 1987 (Oxford University Press in Canada). Every corporate communicator should either hire a crisis manager to construct a written plan or buy these books—preferably both.

To whet the appetite for *pre*-crisis management, I will briefly compare a well-handled crisis to a poorly handled one. Fink's account of the Tylenol incident and Irvine's account of the Challenger explosion serve quite well.

Can You Schedule Your Crisis?

Hardly. But that's no reason not to plan many of your actions in advance. Dozens of tasks that will have to be performed during any type of crisis can be anticipated. These generic duties can be planned to conserve time during the crisis.

Many of us keep flashlights in our car, home or cottage. Crisis management is simply buying flashlights, checking the batteries, deciding what strategic locations they should be in, and so on.

The pre-facto work pays dividends in public confidence, faster recovery and profits. Long after the crisis has past, the media will continue to judge you based on your treatment of them during a crisis.

A crisis is a turning point for better or for worse. The crisis manager tries to make it for the better to reduce the negative impact. In Chinese, the word for crisis is "Wei'Ji", which is two words: danger and opportunity. Proper crisis management reduces the danger and increases the opportunity.

One dangerous myth is that crisis management is new. It has always been practiced; it's just getting more sophisticated. Consider how far airlines have come. In the early days of air travel, newsreel photographers liked to shoot dignitaries or Hollywood stars waving from the stairs of planes. PR people got the good idea of painting the airline's name over the door, in order to get the free publicity. But in the event of a crash, the first airline representative to arrive on the scene knew to carry a bucket of white paint to obliterate the name before the photographers showed up. That was crisis management. Today it's two copies of a three-ring binder with such obscure facts as the nearest 24-hour crane operator.

Tylenol

In the fall of 1982 somebody put cyanide in Tylenol capsules, resealed the packages, and replaced them on shelves in pharmacies and food stores in Chicago. Seven people died. Tylenol is made by McNeil Consumer Products whose parent company is Johnson and Johnson. Without a detailed crisis plan, executives had to scramble for home phone numbers and even the names of people they wanted to contact.

Imagine the shock. J&J is in the health care business, but suddenly was being associated with deaths. Products designed for healing were killing people. Even without a written crisis management plan, J&J instinctively started doing the right thing. An alert PR staffer notified senior management of out-of-the-ordinary interest being shown by a *Chicago Tribune* reporter about Tylenol, J&J and McNeil. As soon as it was determined he was looking into a possible link between Tylenol and a recent death, senior management started to act. A helicopter was hired, facts were gathered, and McNeil's Chairman Dave Collins was put in charge. Collins identified three priorities: 1) stop the killings, 2) come up with a reason for the killings, 3) provide assistance to those in trouble.

While Collins worked, Tylenol became front page news. One study showed 90 per cent of America knew about the deaths within the first week of the crisis. One newspaper columnist called it 'one of the most heavily covered news events since Vietnam'. Yet J&J saved Tylenol, recaptured 98 per cent of its former market and emerged a stronger company with almost no lasting side-effects. J&J had recognized the crisis quickly, established a crisis management team which focused strictly on the crisis and maintained open communications with all concerned.

One moment, when it all could have gone the other way, tells a tale of the value of knowing how media people work and how to work with, not against them. Early in the crisis, reporters wanted to know the answer to an obvious question—Was there cyanide at any Tylenol plants or facilities? J&J VP of Public Relations, Lawrence Foster, checked and said there was no cyanide. Three days later an Associated Press reporter called Foster on a Saturday night to confirm that there was indeed cyanide at McNeil. Foster checked again only to find out he'd been wrong the first time and cyanide could be found on the premises.

What to do was a formidable test of the corporate communicator. Foster called back and told the truth, but went on to point out that cyanide was only used in quality assurance testing, was housed in a completely separate facility, was kept only in small quantities and was all accounted for. It was impossible that any could have gotten into the capsules. Moreover, Foster asked for and received a pledge of secrecy from the reporter on the condition that Foster would release the reporter from the deal if any other media outlet got wind of the story. This worked because it was early in the crisis and J&J was perceived as a victim too. The reporter didn't want to help create panic. The issue was contained.

Forty years before the Tylenol crisis, the late Robert Wood Johnson, son of the founder of J&J enumerated four responsibilities of the company. *In order* they are:

1. to the consumers
2. to the employees
3. to the communities they serve
4. to the stockholders

Hindsight shows that all the swift, effective and compassionate actions taken during the Tylenol crisis were true to these well articulated values.

The Challenger Explosion

What happened at 73 seconds into the 25th space shuttle mission was an unthinkable human tragedy. January 28, 1986 was also an unfortunate and humble end to 25 years of highly successful corporate communications by NASA.

NASA's charter has always stated that any employee may speak to the press or public without fear of retribution. The agency is open, accessible and friendly with the media. For 25 years, it helped create 'space junkies' in the media. This policy paid dividends in budgets, public acceptance and political support.

All this good will evaporated on that January 28th when NASA scheduled and then postponed press briefings on the explosion. The 4 ½ hour delay irreparably damaged media relations. The height of bitter irony is that NASA has had a plan in place since 1983, but did not follow it.

The Solution

A blue print for a successful crisis management plan involves three broad categories: evaluation, compilation and communication. The first requires a good crisis manager to take a hard look at his/her organization's weak points and evaluate vulnerabilities. Simple questions quantify the need:

1. What is a crisis for you? Is it getting your name in print, or not getting your name in print? An inability to continue the enterprise? Three angry phone calls or a chewing out by your boss?
2. What is the likelihood of a crisis occurring?
3. What type of crisis will it be?
4. How intense will it get, how quickly and for how long?
5. What degree of intensity can you, your colleagues and your organization endure and for how long?
6. How interested will the media, government, regulatory bodies and protest groups be in your plight? (A search of similar experiences will help).
7. Will you be the cause or the victim of the crisis?

Chances are you'll find the profile of organizations subject to a long crisis includes those which are public, government, highly visible or with a highly visible CEO, a critical industry or an entity with parallel problems in a 'sister' or related field. The situations which lead to a crisis include loss of life, panic, demonstrated weakness or vacillation, perceived weakness, moral offences, conspiracies, bribes, misuse of public funds or situations which make good media copy.

Musing about these possibilities might lead to the following questions:

1. Who would be your spokespeople?
2. How much could they say?
3. Where would media calls go?
4. Who would handle the media?
5. Where would briefings be held and how often?

If these questions are answered with "don't know" or "not sure", it may be the needed catalyst for more planning. All attempts should be made to quantify the 'guesstimates' used to determine the possibility of a crisis. You will need to look for high impact and high probability areas (i.e. potential big problems tomorrow, not unlikely small problems down the line). Searching for ways to do business even in a crisis and paying more attention to the minor crisis that can lead to a major one, are the first concrete steps you may take after this exercise.

In a big crisis, the main communications target will be the press. Get to know the leaders, talk to them about their needs and perceptions. Be sure of what you're saying and say it with confidence. Be very careful with good news and, above all, be honest.

Finally...

In reviewing the many examples of crisis detailed in these books, I am struck by two things. First, you *can* plan for the future. It just takes long hours of work. This work should be done and it pays dividends. Second, the best plan in the world is no substitute for the right attitude. It may seem old fashioned, but you can't go far wrong telling the truth, kicking a difficult question up the line and keeping the people you serve foremost on your priority list. Good will, support, profits, market share and other benefits will follow naturally.

MASTERING THE PUBLIC PLATFORM

I am nostalgic about this article from Bout de Papier. *It is partly a result of my developing a public speaking course for senior military officers at the height of the Cold War. They had to speak in hostile audiences about the value of alliances (NATO, OAS, NORAD), cruise missile testing, peacekeeping, the nuclear deterrent, and many other contentious issues.*

Public speaking can be dangerous. The Department of National Defense Speakers' Bureau has a trophy they give out to the speaker who does the best that year in an adversarial crowd. The trophy contains a tooth embedded in plexiglass. Legend has it the tooth was knocked out of a Colonel by the proverbial little old lady who didn't like his speech in a church basement.

My research on public speaking for DND also became this article, which I think stands up well 20 years after its writing.

William Henry Harrison, the 9th President of the United States got up on his inaugural day, gave the longest speech to date, caught a cold and died. He's the only person I know of who actually died from speaking in public. But most of us have felt close on many occasions.

In fact, psychologists say that public speaking is our number one fear. Dying is number seven. If this means that people would rather die than speak in public, it explains the large fees that professional speakers are able to command.

There are other rewards for effective public speakers. Who would argue with the contention that Churchill's oratory helped win World War II? Who would argue with John Kennedy's remark that Churchill marshalled the English language and sent it off to war?

Studies show that effective public speakers win respect and visibility, earn raises, promotions and other financial benefits, build power and success for themselves and their organizations and are strong and successful managers and executives. Almost all overcome fear and other barriers to develop their abilities. Effective speaking and presenting don't come naturally to anyone; they take training and practice. In the same way that an experienced executive should never issue a signed memo, report or letter without reading and editing it, a speech or presentation should never be given without adequate rehearsal.

My clients in the military tell me that "time spent in reconnaissance is seldom wasted". Nowhere is this more true than in public presentations. You must find out about any possible sources of resistance to your presentation and the social chatter topics at coffee breaks in order to build bridges. You have to ask yourself what you want your audience to do when you're finished. Too may speakers go the way of Chinese food after an hour. An effective public speaker is like the famous 'tiny time-release pills'. Little ideas stay with the audience, linger, and even days later are released to provoke thought and action. One simple way to achieve this is to end the presentation with the challenge, "So next time you see news reports about topic X, remember my main points today, which are A, B and C".

In order to hold an audience's attention and motivate them to do something or see things your way, one must remember two old clichés of education which are as true as they are hackneyed: 'start where the student is' and 'tell them what you're going to tell them, tell them, then tell them what you've told them.' Many clients have heard these expressions many times, but are still unable to put them into practice. The reason is that they fail to remember that a speech is not a memo, report, performance appraisal, letter or poem. It's a different form of communication requiring different skills—oral not written skills. The spoken word is said and gone, so beginning with the listeners' experience, building bridges to new ideas and repetition for clarity and emphasis are not just highly important, but obligatory.

A good speaker must focus on the benefits the audience will derive from listening and agreeing to the point of view being expressed. Good speakers offer direction, relate to the audience personally, and urge them to act. The vast majority of business meetings, presentations and even speeches are boring, and the audience remembers little and does nothing when they're finished. The challenge is to construct a message that doesn't fall into this category.

Margaret Bedrosian in *Speak Like a Pro* (Wiley, Toronto 1987) offers a checklist for preparing a speech. It should be used by beginners and all of us who have ever had problems with presentation. It's good to go through all the steps and wait for proficiency to develop before cutting out any procedures.

- Write the closing 'call to action' first.
- Write a high impact opening to get the audience's attention.
- Outline the key points of the body of the speech.
- Research (facts, statistics, quotes, examples, anecdotes).
- Put the research where it will support the key points.
- Write out the full text of the speech.
- Rehearse out loud and change any clumsy language.
- Audio tape the next rehearsal for time (add 30 percent to rehearsal time to judge actual performance time).
- Listen to the tape several times (this is excellent practice for timing, pitch, emphasis and other elements that you just can't get any other way).
- *Turn the speech back into notes*—no one reads well. Even if you're a diplomat, and the press and world leaders hang on your every word, and you need a written record, avoid the written scripts at all costs.
- Audio tape and rehearse the notes—try headings in the upper case with lower case points below.
- Prepare any visual aids needed—be sure they're needed because the audience came to see you. They can watch TV or a movie on their own time.

- Write your own introduction—probably the best advice going. It avoids embarrassing moments between you and your host/chair and gets you presented exactly the way you want.

The raw material is now in place, but the reconnaissance is still not over. It's important to visit the room or hall long before the event. Even if it's your own familiar board room, make sure everything works (lights, microphone, visuals, because if anything is going to go wrong, it will be on the day of your presentation). Unfamiliar rooms should be checked for acoustics, seating plans (can you be seen and can you see the audience?), non-smoking areas and ventilation. The room should be uncomfortably cool to allow for body heat to warm it up. If you have any influence over the seating, remember, audiences like lots of aisles. A back section should be roped off for stragglers, to cause audience members to move to the front. Guard your notes and visuals. Many well-meaning custodians or audience members have looked over a speaker's slides and notes and got them out of order at the last minute. Finally, lessen any barriers between you and the audience. Podiums and microphones are the worst offenders.

In a small board room try to stand to command attention. You may need a good excuse like a flip chart or visual aid, but you need to take control and keep it.

Language

We listen and learn visually more than verbally, so a good speaker must create effective 'word pictures' in the listener's mind. Because a speech isn't print, we must use simple, clear language—the old rule of journalism, 'one thought – one sentence' applies to speeches as well. Audiences react well to rhetorical questions, anecdotes and examples. Males especially must remember to avoid sexist language.

Gestures

Gestures are a must. They don't have to be big or theatrical. You don't need many, but you must have them. In oral communication we have no punctuation. Our gestures must supply the commas, periods, dashes and parentheses. Victor Borge's classic comedy routine, where he gives punctuation appropriate sounds and reads a passage complete with audible punctuation, won't work for you, but gestures will. Practicing in front of a mirror or video camera helps and will add to everyone's communications ability.

Know the Audience

The reason for doing all the reconnaissance is to know your audience and venue. The audience co-creates the speech with you. Each speech is different, even if the material is the same. Many novice speakers get nervous because they think the audience wants them to fail for some perverse reason. This isn't true. Most audiences are made up of busy people who don't want to be bored. They want a good presentation and will meet you half way.

Audiences expect polish. Nobody will accept someone getting up and saying the old line, "unaccustomed as I am..." These days everyone's job is to get accustomed. Audiences have different listening and thinking styles. You'll soon be able to recognize the mover, the arranger, the visionary, and the people-relater and use appropriate bridges to each.

The audience's natural state is boredom. They're used to passive entertainment on TV and at the movies, and you have to be able to break down that barrier. People have physical, mental, and chemical distractions. If someone leaves the room (it may be nature or a phone call), don't take it personally or let it throw you. All audiences respond more to less. However long you are asked to speak, speak for 20 per cent less and no one will ever complain. Finally, audiences need to know what to do next—clap, laugh, leave. Good speakers telegraph with body language and key words. Near the end of your speech, if you say "in conclusion" everyone will know to applaud after the next long pause. Take command of the room and the audience will do what you want them to do.

The Rule of 12

You'll be judged by the first 12 steps you take, the first 12 words you say, and the first 12 inches from the top of the head down. Some call this the "take charge opening".

If you're being introduced, you're also being judged by your body language. Be alive and erect. Walk to the podium with determination, pause, make eye contact and start. You've arrived early and perhaps even practiced walking to the lectern and have rehearsed your visuals to ensure they are visible from all parts of the room.

When speaking, it's useful to be able to vary the rate, pitch, tone, and volume of your voice. Tape recording will hone this skill. Articulation and pronunciation increase in importance with audience size. Some words get muffled at the back. One highly underused verbal weapon is silence. In the right place it commands attention.

Ironically, speaking is a real workout. The fittest people need to be extra vigilant in their exercise to maintain a demanding speaking schedule. It's a high energy occupation and you need the reserve energy to turn on the "1000-watt light bulbs" behind your eyes to invigorate a large group.

Recovering from Problems

Even when you've researched, rehearsed and arrived early, there are bound to be problems. Half of what you have to fear is fear itself. This can be eliminated by remembering that no audience cares about the little mistakes. Small errors of grammar, ems, uhs, and repetition aren't noticed in spoken communication. Don't get hung up on them and the listeners won't either.

The huge mistakes, a gravy boat in the lap, a lost speech, or a preceding speaker who has stolen your thunder are big problems. Just remember what fabulous stories they'll make a year later, and try to survive.

Cut your speech short if a large percentage of the group has been drinking. Don't insult drunks. Assume your audience is conservative, so avoid risqué jokes. Be human, especially about your own mistakes.

MECHANICS OF MEDIA RELATIONS

I'm still not sure of the value of conducting a writing course in the public sector. I am constantly told that there are rules that must be followed, such as putting the Minister's name in the first line of a press release. There is no such rule. It is only perceived and received.

A writing course that teaches putting the most newsworthy item at the top of a news release is doomed. Participants say their supervisors will veto short sentences, grabby quotes and interesting statistics in favor of the Minister's name. Yet, I've worked for many Ministers who either don't read all of the hundreds of releases their department issues each year, or don't care if their name is at the top.

I have often said that there'd be a great story if a journalist obtained all the "track changes" made by senior administrators on a mundane press release. The journalist could then estimate what it cost the taxpayer to write and rewrite this item, and could report on what the communications shop could have done more efficiently without this "help".

Note the dig on planning at the end. I found out, almost 20 years after writing this, that business

Professor Henry Mintzberg has a similar aversion to planning—the illusion of doing something.

At any rate, I think this old column from Bout de Papier *still presents a valuable lesson.*

I would love to meet the civil servants who troll the halls of government departments inspecting press releases to make sure they're boring. They must exist, because the average public sector press release reads like this:

FREDERICTON, N.B., Feb 12, 1998:

The Hon. H.E.M. Locke, federal minister responsible for trees and member for Whispering Pine, Ontario, along with the Hon. Bruce Spudworm, provincial minister responsible for land and the member for Dulce Bay announced today a federal/provincial cost sharing agreement to stimulate and advance the scientific...

BO-RING! I have asked why they don't try something like this: "I'm delighted with the progress we've made", says the Hon. H.E.M. Locke...

My clients in the federal public sector say they actually must follow written guidelines that require writing in this style. Yet at least one person in the Privy Council Office says no such guidelines exist and if they do, they do not have to be followed verbatim. Somebody isn't talking to somebody.

One federal agency told me they send out 200 press releases a year and not one is picked up by the media. The result is often waste and a message which does not reach the public. There are better ways to write a press release and promote productive relations with the media.

The Release

William Parkhurst (*How to Get Publicity*, Times Books, 1985) is right when he says the press release is the most important document in your media relations strategy. He suggests the writer start by asking a lot of questions that begin with the traditional 5 Ws and H. Who will benefit? What is being done that's new? When will results show? Where will be the greatest impact? Why is this being done now? How will it work?

There's more to it than Parkhurst suggests though. Having articulated all the elements of the story, these must be sifted through a matrix of standard journalistic criteria such as timeliness, proximity, number of people affected, lasting importance and so on. Generally, stories which are brand new, nearby, affect many people, and will have lasting historical importance are the most newsworthy. The point is illustrated by gauging the changing importance of a seemingly inconsequential two car fender-bender outside a radio and TV station in a big city. It doesn't sound newsworthy, but add some of the following elements and the situation changes:

1. It happened 30 seconds before news time and a reporter happened to get a great sound recording of the cars colliding.
2. One of the drivers was dressed as a clown on his way to the circus.
3. One car was a police cruiser.
4. It happened two nights ago, but there is a spectacular film of the cars colliding and knocking over the TV reporter.
5. It happened 10 years ago.
6. It happened 10 years ago, and it has just come to light that one of the drivers was Pierre Trudeau.
7. It happened 10 years ago. One driver was former Prime Minister Pierre Trudeau and the other was Prime Minister Brian Mulroney.

You have a picture. Call the *New York Times*. You're rich!

Most things can be newsworthy in the right context. The communications professional's job is contextualization. The 5 Ws and H must be constantly weighted against standard journalist criteria and competing stories in a moving matrix. Highlight one aspect and play down another. It is like juggling on roller skates on a moving train. When you get it right, you're not only having fun, but really going places too.

Having decided the most newsworthy angle, you must write a lead, or first sentence. Parkhurst lists some of the types including the question, quotation and humorous leads. There are also shotgun, rifle, umbrella, split, historical, geographic and others detailed in any good journalistic style book.

I agree with whoever said that good writing is just good talking put on paper. One thought per sentence, present tense, active voice and the transmission of simple word pictures are the foundation of clear communication. The release must have a straight spine. The writer must be taking the reader someplace and not deviate. You must start at A and logically end at Z and not divert to math when you promised to deliver the alphabet. This concept of simplicity, or 'journalism as a form letter' is the hardest concept for students of journalism or PR to grasp. They all want to be Hemmingway because he once wrote news.

Above all, ask yourself, "who cares?" If you can't picture a nurse, policeman, taxi driver, unemployed laborer, professor or others being interested, then re-write it. So, instead of writing "A Canadian traveler was rescued by a consular official..." you might try, "Joe Smith, who normally handles minor passport and visa problems for Canadians abroad, became a hero to at least one family today..."

Format

There is a study I like to cite that shows that the average human resources manager looks at the average unsolicited resumé for 14 seconds. I suspect the same is true of press releases. A stack of one hundred releases in newsrooms where I used to work was not uncommon, but neither was the fact that 90 of them were single spaced, had no date, had no contact person, were boring or had other faults that eliminated them from contention. Basic format rules are as follows:

1. Leave generous margins all around.
2. Use your organization's letterhead, not special news release stationary.
3. Banish mundane procedural data and get quickly into the headline and body.
4. Type 'for immediate release' or 'not for release before 2 p.m.' and date in the upper right hand corner. Don't squander your 14 seconds in extraneous facts.
5. Use a short, grabby headline typed in capitals.
6. Write in conversational, journalistic style (consult a style book).
7. Avoid boring details. Try starting with a quote and list dates, places and other details further down.

8. Double or triple space.

9. Tell the whole story, even if it takes 2 or 3 pages. (It will be thrown out if you haven't interested the reporter in the first paragraph, but having done so, you must do a complete job).

10. End with the traditional marks -30- followed by 'for further information contact Fred Bloggins...' and a phone number.

Hooks

If the editor looks up from your release and asks, "What does this have to do with the price of tea in China?", you don't have a hook. Hooks are reasons for doing the story, today, in this way. Unusual things, human interest and striking photographs are special cases where the hook may be the story itself. A two-headed calf story is news anytime and has to run when discovered.

Obvious hooks are the piggyback kind. National implications of local stories, local angles to international stories, and your reaction to a continuing story are examples. The easiest are time hooks. A calendar will give you lots of story ideas. People travel at Christmas, March break and in the summer. They start school in September and end it in April or June. There is more unemployment in the winter than in the summer and seasonal types of employment at all times. The weather patterns change about every 3 months and there are a couple of dozen holidays or anniversaries per year. Your organization can plug into a good dozen of these events and piggyback on existing media awareness/interest. In this way you may even be able to make routine releases of upcoming events, personnel changes, and statements of positions interesting.

What Else Do You Send?

Releases do not take the place of media tours, private interviews, public service announcements, background briefings, conferences, letters to the editor, and other tools. Moreover, the mailing of a release is a good excuse to send other material. A recent clipping about your organization or on a topic related to your release signals to the media that you are newsworthy. Biographies, cover letters, fact sheets, transcripts of recent electronic interviews, photos, lists of recent media appearances, company brochures or annual reports all can make a professional press kit.

To the media, a well run communications department signals a well run organization. In times of crisis or controversy, you will be judged, in part, on how professional your communications were during average times.

To Whom Do You Send?

"But we always send to the CBC and they never cover us" says a client. "How did you address the release?" I ask. "The Editor, CBC, Box 500 Stn. A, Toronto", says the complaining client.

The Canadian Broadcasting Corporation has a huge building in Toronto, housing AM, FM, TV, French and English. Each public affairs show has an 'editor', as do the national radio and TV and local radio and TV newsrooms. You need to send 15 news releases to CBC alone. There are also 1,500 other AM & FM radio stations in Canada, 130 TV stations, 700 cable systems, 850 weekly newspapers with a circulation of 3.3 million and 116 daily newspapers with 5.5 million readers.

I get frustrated when professional communicators say the media is lazy, out to get them and won't cover their events for ideological reasons, and they say their press list contains 80 names for the whole country. Media bashing is a smoke screen for inaction.

Media 'Etiquette'

Parkhurst actually breaths a little life into the old cliché of the freeloading reporter who shows up to the press conference because there is food. There may also be crooked politicians, bureaucrats who sleep on the job and industrialists who knowingly poison ground water. But what do these clichés tell us about effective media, government, or industrial relations? Just to put the chestnut to rest, when a journalist is covering four stories between 10 a.m. and 4:30 p.m. all over town, s/he often has to eat on the run.

Simple etiquette rules will help your media campaign:

1. Treat reporters like regular people under pressure to get a story.
2. Brief them well. Then do it again.
3. Don't say you have 'news', say you have some information and let the reporter do his/her job in deciding if it is news.

4. Don't thank a reporter. That implies s/he has done you a favor which is unethical. Say his story was interesting, clear or timely.

5. A call before the release goes out to alert the reporter is helpful. A call afterwards is pushy.

Communication Plans

While practitioners should be de-mystifying the media relations process for senior managers, there is too often a sense that more gobbledygook and planning is an end in itself. Planning has its place but the fact is often forgotten, that planning is not actually doing anything. It is just planning to do something and does not take the place of real and appropriate action. Better to send out one so-so press release than to write up a plan that has 10 full media kits going out each quarter, but is never implemented.

Finally...

The world is as it is—not as it should be. The media, warts and all, exist. Don't waste time trying to reform the media—change your approach. The newsmakers' job is to know everything about media deadlines, style, foibles, values, ethics, needs and what makes news. All the rest is just plain work.

PRESIDENT CLINTON'S HARD WORK

This is one of my most recent columns, and illustrates the timeless theme of how hard work produces results. How many executives or lower level politicians would dedicate the amount of time to rehearsal and practice that President Clinton did?

Results are usually commensurate with input.

I am fortunate to have just been a guest at the Bill Clinton Presidential Library in Little Rock, Arkansas. It's a magnificent building, jutting out of a brown field site toward the river, parallel to a rusty old railway bridge.

The President's accomplishments are chronicled in the context of the times. Bill and Hillary's talents are showcased via the short films they made spoofing popular culture (Forest Gump, etc.). The President's appearances at annual White House correspondents dinners rival almost any President's ability to demonstrate ease and wit.

Then there are the actual texts of his speeches, complete with hand-written edits. It's easy to tell that Bill Clinton did a lot of his own writing and made changes right up until delivery time. A lesson for all speechwriters and politicians is that he removed redundancies and excess verbiage ("if I might," etc.). He would have sounded stilted if he'd delivered this kind of boiler-plate.

One display highlighted a State of the Union address. For this one occasion, the President's schedule shows at least three meetings and revisions to at least three drafts and memos over 10 days.

Then he had three rehearsal sessions totaling nine hours. This was followed by an all day rehearsal on the day of the address. No wonder he did well in the 55 minute speech!

How many politicians rehearse this much for their all candidates meetings and televised debates? How many CEOs rehearse this much for analysts' calls?

There no big secret to being good at communication. It's work!

INTERVIEW TIPS FROM THE CAMPAIGN TRAIL

I quickly wrote this piece on deadline for The Globe and Mail. *The piece would have been unusable the day after the election. The comparison between a campaign and a job interview is valid in every jurisdiction and election. If you've long forgotten the foibles of these candidates, or even some of the candidates themselves, the principles are still valid.*

Conservative Stephen Harper won a minority government and Liberal Prime Minister Paul Martin retired, causing a leadership convention. New Democrat Jack Layton on the left still leads his party, as does separatist Gilles Duceppe.

The interview process (election) could begin again at any moment.

Four politicians just finished a long job interview of sorts with Canadian electors. Workers in the job market can learn some lessons about how to conduct themselves in real job interviews by studying the four major party leaders' styles in their campaigns, and how those would translate to the workplace.

Gilles Duceppe

In walks a sort of likeable, presentable guy who seems smart. But early in the interview, he lets it be known that he's in charge, not you. He will only work at one of your plants, has no interest in several of your product lines, doesn't think you're even in the right business, and wants to start up his own competing operation after getting experience with you anyway.

Real-life job candidates should show knowledge of the employer, but not insult the potential boss and HR manager by being too proscriptive on how to run the operation. Reading company web sites, annual reports and even brochures is a good place to start finding information about the company, but beware of simply parroting the buzz words you might find in some of the literature. Make sure instead that you understand substantive issues, such as earnings, distribution issues and the corporate culture.

This way you show initiative, but don't send out signals that you want to immediately change an already successful company. An insulting way to show initiative would be to start saying, "Professional HR departments should…" or "A modern company must…" Use instead phrases such as "I'd like to learn more about…" or "I hope my contribution would be…" This shows your willingness to be a team player.

Also, interviewers are on the lookout for candidates who are more interested in their well being than the company's. One way candidates can do this is by hijacking the interview with discussions about their own interests that have nothing to do with the goals of the company. An interview can often include discussions of personal activities, but should show stability and commitment, and not overshadow the business end of the discussion.

Stephen Harper

You've seen this candidate before. He was a bit of a know-it-all in the last interview and even prickly. And he had some radical views that worried you. But he seemed worth another look.

This time he has grown and polished his interview skills. He's clean cut and serious, and even has a nice new hairdo. He appears to be a hard worker. In the interview he lists a lot of ideas right off the bat. You might not want to have a beer after work with the guy, but you feel comfortable that he can run the regional office and you can trust him to deal with details like inventory, just-in-time delivery and complex legal issues.

In real life, candidates must be on their best behavior in job interviews. They don't have to come across as someone the interviewers would want as a friend, but prospective employers expect a polished, rehearsed performance in the initial encounter. If they don't get it, they will assume that a prickly and opinionated performance in an interview will give them a prickly and opinionated employee.

Serious candidates for all levels of jobs run through mock-interviews and study their video taped performances. Studies show that ambiguous body language (fidgeting, eye-rolling, leg crossing, etc.) is interpreted negatively. Also, a tendency to talk too much, correct interviewers, snap back or look superior will annoy interviewers. Listen carefully to independent critiques of your mock interviews. A general rule is "suffer fools gladly" and tone everything down 30 per cent.

Candidates can come across as hard workers by sincerely stating what they like about their work. Managers can talk about developing young workers' potential. Accountants can enjoy the symmetry of good books, and even warehouse supervisors can talk about the peace of mind they get from knowing where everything is.

Most people have potentially embarrassing things in their past, such as unguarded comments in a personal blog. These things are so easy to search today that candidates must be prepared to discuss why they posted the opinions they did on issues such as same-sex marriage, guns or abortion. If asked, one defense might be that you were young but have matured since then. If the writing or design was good, you can point out your communications skills. You can also suggest that the matter does not reflect on the workplace. But the best defense is scouring the Internet or other public sources and doing what you can to get rid of inappropriate items.

Jack Layton

This guy comes out with lots of ideas and has a series of decent answers to the first round of questioning. But then he starts sounding more interested in the customer than the company's interest.

"I'm totally focused on customers," he says. "In fact, I want to get things done for young customers, the elderly customers, customers who are in school, ordinary customers, working customers, customers who come from the same family and customers who no one else will help serve".

If you get too focused on one stakeholder, the interviewers may start wondering whether you have a good grasp of the totality of the company. One good technique is to illustrate how you have balanced competing interests in the past, perhaps with regulators, customers, suppliers and unionized workers. If there was a happy result or unexpected solution you worked out, you'll be signaling that you can handle complex issues productively without stepping on toes.

But when discussing your ideas, don't lecture your potential new boss about how the company has been doing things wrong for many years. This is a tacit criticism of the company and can sound holier-than-thou. You may have the company's best interests at heart, but still sound too preachy and eager. Instead, take a more humble approach and talk about how you are eager to tackle some of the issues, products or territory this new position requires.

Paul Martin

Here's an older candidate who appears to have the experience and energy to do the job. But he's too energetic and anxious at times— he's waving his arms and sweeping the room with his eyes and not making eye contact. Perhaps he really needs the job and he's trying hard to convince you to give it to him and not someone else.

He does have a wonderful resumé. He's entrepreneurial, and has held senior positions in the past. The question is whether he can do the job again.

Then he starts to attack other candidates. "I think you should know that my fundamental values are quite different than the other candidates' values," he says.

Serious candidates make efforts to control their nerves before a big job interview. Arriving early in the city or neighborhood, going for a walk and not overeating all help. So does avoiding distractions such as phone calls and spread sheets in the hours before the interview. A calm, confident person can better maintain eye contact and alert body language with one person at a time. To stay calm, a candidate can remember to breathe, take a pause before answering questions and remember to sit comfortably in a chair. This way s/he won't look either too rigid or fidgety, which makes a candidate seem anxious.

Even well-qualified candidates can't rely totally on past performance. Successful business people have to prove themselves every day. They can't rest on their laurels and must show they crave the next challenge. This interview is all about the candidate demonstrating he can perform in the future. More talk about what he can and will do, rather than what he did do in the past is advisable.

This candidate is making a mistake by trying to get points through attacking other candidates, especially by comparing his values with theirs. Human resources professionals and senior managers don't scare easily and want specific skills and ideas from candidates. You don't hire someone simply because he says the other candidates are bad. In fact, attacking other candidates may make interviewers wonder whether you might badmouth their company in the future. Instead, stick to talking about your own skills and why you would make the best candidate for the job.

And when you talk about yourself and your values, remember that people with strong ethics can talk very specifically about what they've done to illustrate the point, and don't need to trumpet generalities.

A job interview is really a short test of what it will be like to have you around 50 hours a week for a few years. The candidate can't be too opinionated, prickly or angry.

On election day, voters choose the candidate they feel performed best over the course of this long process with the public. The candidate selection process, including media scrutiny and the rubber chicken circuit is a great job interview.

The Top Ten Lessons Learned
in the Canadian Election

This is from my running blog during the last Canadian election. The lessons are generic, so if you've long forgotten last year's issue, or don't know the candidates, the issues are worth a quick read regardless.

1. **In Politics and in Life You Must Campaign as if You Were Down 15 Points and the Outcome of the Election Would Change Your Family's Lifestyle for Generations. Why?**

   a) That just might be the case.

   b) All organizations need to exercise the troops—you might need them mid-term for an initiative, or for the next election.

   c) In the Parliamentary system you are also campaigning for cabinet, and if you're the leader, you are campaigning to keep your troops in line when you win. Wide winning margins accomplish both goals.

2. **You Have to Show Growth and the Ability to Deal with the Unforeseen.**

Voters saw the best that NDP leader Jack Layton and Liberal Prime Minister Paul Martin had to offer in the first few weeks—and it was pretty good. Conservative leader Harper was not as good, but did show that he had some room to improve and grow. He grew through rehearsal and practice. He reaped the benefits. Voters will expect more growth in the future.

3. Voters Defeat More Governments Than They Elect.

It's not that the electorate has warmed to Stephen Harper. It's that the electorate could not continue to be warm to Liberal Paul Martin. Stephen Harper still has to win over Canadians, even as Prime Minister.

4. Generalizations Don't Work in the Long Run—the Electorate has a Tendency to Vote for Specifics.

All parties were abjectly guilty of using vacuous slogans. The Conservatives "Stand Up For Canada", the NDP's "Getting Results For People", and the Liberals "Choose Your Canada" are not any more empty than Prime Minister Lester Pearson's "Sixty Days of Decision" or Prime Minister Trudeau's "Just Society" from the 1960s and 70s. But times have changed. Media saturation and multiple-sources of information mean the electorate can get tired of slogans more quickly.

Slogans will get attention, but then the voter wants the payoff for paying attention—specifics.

The electorate knows situations can change after election day. But the candidate who has firm positions for the issues that arise during a campaign is deemed to be the one who will have something specific to do when governing and dealing with unforeseen issues.

5. American Techniques do not Translate Well into the Canadian Parliamentary System.

A Governor in Texas spends $30 million US to get there. Many Senators spend about that to get re-elected. A Canadian or provincial leader might spend between a few hundred thousand to a couple of million in special cases. A provincial or federal riding or district has a spending limit imposed on it of less than $90,000 Canadian, diminishing in smaller ridings.

Canadian campaigns last for weeks, whereas American campaigns last for months and Presidential campaigns almost never end.

Anyone expecting US style negative ads to work in Canada hasn't done proper homework.

Techniques that can work well in a two-party system do not necessarily translate into a three party system with at least one strong regional party.

6. N>P

A negative is greater than a positive—meaning more memorable. It was Prime Minister Paul Martin who actually highlighted improprieties by appointing the Gomery Commission and touring the country talking about corruption—a big mistake.

7. You Can Never Let Your Guard Down.

Stephen Harper helped erode his own lead in the final days with American political terms such as "checks and balances" and reference to a Liberal Senate and judiciary limiting his power should he get a majority. We do not have the separation of powers that the US system has. We do not combine head of government and head of state. Our judges don't run for office on their records. Our Senate does not "advise and consent" as the US Senate does, but provides "sober second thought"—which is often neither. The US-style reference opened up the fears that Harper is a US-style neo-con, which is not true, but damaging nonetheless.

8. Don't Distract Yourself and Your Organization From the Task at Hand.

Prime Minister Martin's "notwithstanding clause" constitutional gambit was a huge diversion that sapped energy and focus from the core task of getting elected. Canadians don't focus on constitutional matters. It did not smoke out Conservative Leader Harper on same-sex marriage and abortion because it was too complex a series of leaps of logic to understand that point anyway. And, an act of Parliament forbidding the federal government from using the clause could be rescinded by any future Parliament. A constitutional amendment forbidding the clause's use would need support from 7 provinces with 50 per cent of the population. This route would have to be taken if a judge were persuaded that Parliament limiting its powers to use the clause, were also a limit on the Senate's powers—which are enshrined in the Canadian Constitution.

Martin's gambit was a dog's breakfast, at best.

9. You Must Have a Thorough Understanding of Core Issues.

Judicial appointments being political, Senate limits on the Prime Minister's power, and the "notwithstanding clause" gambit, all showed that both Conservative Leader Harper and Liberal Prime Minister Martin did not fully think through these statements. Our judges are indeed political appointees, but are immediately thereafter untouchable by politicians. The Senate is no effective check on a Prime Minister or Parliament's power.

10. You Have to Possess Basic Skills.

Athletes need cardio-vascular endurance, flexibility, strength and anaerobic explosive power. Corporate executives need to know how to read a financial statement, work a room and schmooze with the press. Political teams need to know both clean and dirty tricks to get elected.

- Stephen Harper's MA thesis in economics should not have been readily available in the University of Calgary library.

- The Conservatives' negative ad, attacking NDP Leader Layton, was too personal, anatomical (using his moustache!), not well shot and ineffective.

- The Liberals should not have commissioned, let alone released, 11 attack ads all in one day. That alone would have scuttled the technique. Hyperbole, errors, being too negative, too personal and too irrelevant, killed the effort.

Ad Hominem

Below is a compilation of thoughts from my interactive blog during the Liberal Convention which
chose Stéphane Dion as leader. The short
accounts illustrate that politics is all about people.

Ken Dryden

I start with the former star goalie for the fabled Montreal Canadians
because Mr. Dryden has had millions of peoples' rapt attention for
decades. He should know how to work a room. But he's terribly
shy and only started making good speeches near the end of his
leadership campaign.

He was so popular at the convention, that there was a twenty
minute wait to get on the elevator to go up to his hospitality suite.
Once there, the first thing I saw was the candidate sitting at a table
in the hall, as if selling tickets. In a lull in the action, I approached
and said,

"1974, Saint John, New Brunswick, sports celebrity dinner—I interviewed you!"

The candidate stuck out a hand in slow motion, barely caught my
eye and didn't react to my nutty introduction. I wonder how many
hundred of times delegates or potential volunteers introduced
themselves by saying they'd been at a particularly exciting game in
which Mr. Dryden played? He should know how to react by now.

Later, inside, I sat within arm's length of the candidate as he
listened to a guest talk at length. It was so noisy I couldn't hear
what was being said, but did see Mr. Dryden nodding and

contributing about 20 per cent of the conversation. This went on for about ten minutes. When the discussion broke off, I determined that the guest was not a voting delegate and had dubious media credentials.

Successful candidates must be able to make instant contact with people and break off graciously to work a crowded room.

Stéphane Dion

I was in mid-sentence with Don Newman on his CBC Newsworld show "Politics", when the newly elected Liberal leader marched onto the set and was wired up to be interviewed. He had just finished half a dozen other interviews in English and French, yet instantly began a lucid dozen minutes with one of the best political interviewers in the media. Mr. Dion did very well.

What struck me more was what he did when the cameras were off and the show was over. He walked around and shook hands with every camera operator, technician and producer on the set. It was quick, but he got to them all.

I caught the new leader's eye. With a stairway and a railing between us, he had to take a few steps toward me and lean over to hear. It was a bit presumptuous of me to beckon him, but I said the following:

"Stephen Harper [Conservative Prime Minister] would never do that. I've been in TV studios across the country, and camera operators often tell me he snubs them. You did it exactly right".

I, not so jokingly, tell my clients to take a look around the TV set for the person dressed in the worst ripped jeans and wearing a baseball cap. That's probably the most senior person. Introduce yourself to everyone. If they don't like you, they can get you in the edit suite!

Michael Ignatieff

For no particular reason, some have compared the diplomat's son to Pierre Trudeau. Other than short connections to Harvard and being university lecturers, meeting the two is a vastly different experience.

My father had business dealings with Mr. Trudeau in the 1960s in Montreal. He said he'd had innumerable, intense, 90-second encounters with the future Prime Minister. I had a few during his tenure and after. I only rated 30 seconds, but Mr. Trudeau could make you feel like the only person in the room for a short time.

So, when Michael Ignatieff walked within arm's length of me at the convention, I wanted to see how he dealt with that 30-second window.

"I knew your father," I said, as I stuck out my hand.

Being younger than the candidate, this statement intrigued him enough to take two paces toward my hand and shake.

"He was much older" I said.

I mentioned that we'd gone to the same school, years apart, but the famous Canadian diplomat, George Ignatieff, would return for reunions or to speak.

While candidate Ignatieff looked a little intrigued, I did not feel he fully engaged. His body language and facial expressions didn't change much. We had our exchange and off he went.

I wonder how many delegates had a similar perfunctory experience, and whether this accounts for his lack of growth past the first ballot?

Martha Hall Findlay

I didn't encounter the only woman in the race, but one of my researchers did. Amanda Moddejonge made the rounds of hospitality suites after a debate in Toronto. Candidate Hall Findlay's party was sparsely populated, so Ms. Moddejonge should have stood out. Yet the candidate arrived only to schmooze with her own workers, rather than try to find delegates or media to meet.

Working the room is partly a staffer's responsibility, and picking that staffer is entirely the candidate's responsibility. Either way, politics is about people.

EPILOGUE

When we look at the political realities of electoral politics, at least in Canada and United States, the old rules of what it takes to win and the metrics of predicting success have changed. Proof of this can be seen in closeness of the Al Gore's "loss" to George W. Bush in 2000 where Gore won the popular vote but not the Presidency. Howard Dean's rapid rise through the Internet and traditional television fall from grace in mere days shows the volatility of voters' attitudes.

It can also be seen in the recent Liberal Party of Canada's leadership victory by Stéphane Dion, whom few considered as a front-runner before the first ballot. It can even be seen here in my home province, in the surprising victory of the relatively obscure Ed Stelmach, who recently won the leadership of the Alberta Progressive Conservative Party on a one person, one vote model of party members. When the original front runners faltered, voters changed their minds and thousands of new people purchased party memberships during the week before a second ballot, so they could participate. They picked a preferred but relatively unknown alternative, defying the pronouncements of the political and pundit experts in the process.

The reality that most elections are lost and not won is still true. But the factors that now determine the people's choice are no longer tied to the traditional parameters of the past which ironically, continue to preoccupy main-stream media commentators and punditry. Evaluations based on who has the most money and whether it's from powerful sources; who has the charisma or the right political pedigree; who has the top strategists, organizers and the best political "machine"; who is getting the most media coverage; and what the polls say, has become less and less relevant to final election outcomes.

A consequence of this changing political reality is that traditional media and opinion pollsters are often embarrassed by their predictions of who they say will win. This is characteristic of much of the hyper-competitive media market place today, where it has become more important to be first with the news than to be right or accurate. Don't get me wrong; there are excellent individual reporters and columnists who are exceptions to this generalization. There just aren't enough of them, especially given the realities of their mediums and a media culture of instant information and short term attention spans.

The vast array of typical political campaign grist is misinformation, propaganda, rhetoric, dirty tricks, posturing, maneuvering, spin and sloganeering. This is all provided on a constant 24 hour news cycle designed to serve the mainstream media's voracious hunger for content, not necessarily the public's hope for enlightenment. What results is media coverage that leans towards insipid gossip, vacuous feature reports and vapid insight pieces that are more akin to the tabloid coverage of Paris Hilton than a serious political event. This is not at all helpful to engage and inform a citizenry and, in fact, it is toxic and harmful to helping voters to make informed decisions about how they want to be governed–and by whom.

The majority of the population has moved on from that world of political hype and hyperbole. They are turned off by the lack of substance in what they are hearing or the disconnect between their lives and politics or government. Too many citizens reject this status-quo political process and decide to "participate" by staying home on election day. And those who are consciously and conscientiously engaged are less and less influenced by the old style of political campaigning. They are realizing they can't depend on the integrity of the political system, the honesty of campaign content, the methodology of polling, the impartiality of the media, or even the authenticity of the public image of the candidates because they are so carefully packaged and "market-tested for acceptability".

There is a feeling amongst large segments of the public that no one will really help them understand the issues and get to know the candidates or explain the consequences of what is being proposed as preferred public policy. That said then, the understanding of how these citizens make their choices is simply not as cut and dried, nor as predictable, as it used to be. Political predictions are often so uncertain that they are more akin to astrology than any serious discipline or science.

So, if the roles and responsibilities of citizenship are inherent within the political systems, but those systems no longer serve the needs of the citizenry, what is to be done to change things? We can't afford to continue to drive citizens away from their democratic and political participation and to push them to the side lines of the public policy decision making processes. The political systems and institutions are not going to change by themselves. Nothing positive will happen unless the citizenry starts to re-engage in civics and decide that they are taking back the power from the game players and creators of political puppets masquerading as candidates.

Citizens have to start taking their critical civic role and responsibility of choosing their governments and their elected representatives much more seriously and actively. The world is run by those who show up! The fewer that turn out for elections, the greater the concentration of power into the various organized activist and special interests groups who are engaged but often only around single issues.

The result is a reduction in the chances that our politics and governments will actually reflect and respect the broader social interests of citizens. It is an undeniable truth that in a democracy you always get the government you deserve, whether you voted or not. Do we dare leave all that power, influence and authority over us, our families, our enterprises and our communities to someone else because we value cynicism over citizenship?

K.J. (Ken) Chapman
Cambridge Strategies Inc.
2007

3rd Printing – With a New Epilogue by the Author
allan bonner

Praise for

DOING & SAYING THE
RIGHT THING

"It all comes down to messaging and THE SOCKO SYSTEM is the best single volume I have read on how to get your message across as well as what pitfalls we can avoid..."

– Colin Robertson,
Advocacy Minister and head of the
Washington Secretariat,
Embassy of Canada

"I consider myself fortunate to have benefited from being trained in the SOCKO method by Allan Bonner and his team. My training occurred just after my appointment as Canada's chief negotiator for the North American Free Trade Agreement... The common sense SOCKO approach allowed me to think much more clearly about how to communicate, and I am convinced led to a better result both for the government and the media and their audience".

– John M. Weekes, Chairman,
Global Trade Practices, APCO Worldwide,
Geneva

"Over the years, SOCKO has proven to be an effective tool for avoiding the communications pitfalls we all face in an ever interrelated and fast-moving world. In a daily ritual where people are bombarded by sales pitches and spins of all varieties, your training approach can make the difference between 20 seconds of fame and a painful, time-consuming damage control strategy. Yours is ultimately a discipline which enhances the credibility of the message and the messenger".

– Hon. Sergio Marchi, Ambassador,
The Permanent Mission of Canada to the United Nations,
Geneva

"The SOCKO system is a pragmatic, hands-on, must-read book that demonstrates how to refine, hone, and develop your personal communications skills..."

– Major-General Richard Rohmer,
OC, CCM, DFC, O.ONT, K.StJ, CD, QC

184

Praise for

ALLAN BONNER'S
MEDIA RELATIONS

"Allan Bonner's wide experience as a broadcaster and consultant makes this a valuable handbook to understanding the media. It deals clearly and concisely with everything you need to know when you find yourself in the news spotlight...from organizing the press conference, to getting your message across, to answering the tough questions. Essential and Insightful".

– LLOYD ROBERTSON,
CTV NEWS

"Bonner has taken the mystery, and I expect the fear, out of media interviews with this informative tome. By telling the reader in no uncertain terms what the reporter expects, he is making our job as a journalist all the easier. It's a must read for anyone who has to deal with the print, radio or television media".

– HAROLD LEVY,
THE TORONTO STAR

"Truly, a university class in media relations. It's a must read reference source for large and small businesses, governments, schools, and non-profits. Bonner knows what he is talking about, telling the secrets that make dealing with the media easier and more productive".

– JOE BATES,
KVOS TV

"This is an entertaining, common-sense analysis of the right and wrong ways to deal with the media, by a writer who knows his subject intimately and has the war stories to prove it".

– WARREN CLEMENTS, MEMBER OF THE EDITORIAL BOARD,
THE GLOBE AND MAIL

"A simple but all-encompassing guide for those plunged into dealing with the media... The book is a valuable resource".

– HARVEY SCHACHTER, COLUMNIST,
THE GLOBE AND MAIL